Beautiful Gift

Beautiful Gift

How I Found My Son in the Afterlife

Lesa Kay Smith

LKS
Publishing

For Kenny, Jessica, Cody
and
Brandon

Death Is Nothing at All

Death is nothing at all.
I have only slipped away to the next room.
I am I and you are you.
Whatever we were to each other,
That, we still are.

Call me by my old familiar name.
Speak to me in the easy way
which you always used.
Put no difference into your tone.
Wear no forced air of solemnity or sorrow.

Laugh as we always laughed
at the little jokes we enjoyed together.
Play, smile, think of me. Pray for me.
Let my name be ever the household word
that it always was.
Let it be spoken without effect.
Without the trace of a shadow on it.

Life means all that it ever meant.
It is the same that it ever was.
There is absolute unbroken continuity.
Why should I be out of mind
because I am out of sight?

I am waiting for you.
For an interval.
Somewhere. Very near.
Just around the corner.

All is well.
Nothing is hurt; nothing is lost.
One brief moment and all will be as it was before.
How we shall laugh at the trouble of parting when we meet again!

Henry Scott Holland
Regius Professor of Divinity
University of Oxford-1910

I was sitting in the driver's seat of my daughter Jessica's car, my cell phone in one hand and a pen and my small journal in the other. I was staying with Jessica and my son Cody in Scottsdale, Arizona, during our first holiday season without my older son Brandon, who had passed away almost a year ago. I was devastated by my son's death, and as soon as he passed I knew I wanted to try to find him in the afterlife. When I lost my dad more than thirty years ago, I had a vivid dream in which he came to me and told me he was fine. That was my first encounter with someone I loved coming to me from the other side, and ever since then I've had a firm belief that death is not the end and that our loved ones who have passed on go on living in some other place.

But it had taken me a year to locate a medium that I wanted to use to try to make contact with Brandon. A month later I called and with some trepidation made the appointment. Now the day of the appointment had arrived: I was about to call Jamie Butler, a clairvoyant and clairaudient medium who lived in Atlanta.

I'd never tried to contact a loved one who had passed, and I had no idea what to expect or how a meeting with a medium worked. I felt totally apprehensive about what I was going to hear and learn today. But I was determined to find my son. I was shaking when I dialed the number. I heard the phone ring a couple of times.

"Hello," Jamie answered, in a voice so sweet and soothing it put me at ease.

I poured out my reason for calling, being careful not to give away too much information because I wanted to be sure that Jamie was legitimate—that she truly had the rare gift of what used to be called second sight.

"Is my son there?" I asked urgently, suddenly filled with

excitement that I could possibly make contact with Brandon.

"Yes," Jamie said, "he is." Then she went on to say, "I see a gun. Is that what caused your son's death?"

"Yes!" I said my eyes welling up with tears.

And then Jamie said something that was the first of many messages from my son that convinced me it was really him talking, through her, to me. "He's saying, 'Oh Mom, I'm so happy you're doing this so I can tell you that I'm fine." And then Jamie said she saw him on his knees as if he was begging for forgiveness. "I'm so sorry," she said Brandon said. "It was a stupid accident."

CHAPTER 1

THE DARKNESS

It was four in the morning on January 11, 2008, and I was awakened by a loud knock on the door. I had woken up in the night and fallen back to sleep in the recliner in the living room. I stumbled to the door and opened it. Two deputy sheriffs were standing on my front step. I knew the news would not be good, and I didn't want to hear what they had to say. Still, I didn't think they would tell me what they were about to tell me. That knock on the door in the middle of the night always happens to other people. I never thought it would ever, ever happen to me.

"Are you the mother of Brandon Smith?" one deputy asked.

"Yes. Is he okay?"

"No," the deputy answered.

In that moment my heart stopped and I dropped into a horrible place, a nightmare country from which I would never return to the life I took for granted before. Numbness spread throughout my entire body, and I crumbled and fell to the floor crying and weeping and screaming. *I'm going to die,* I thought. *I can't breathe, I can't do this.*

"Could you get your husband?" the deputy asked.

I started screaming my husband's name. "Kenny! Kenny! Get out here! Get out here! It's Brandon."

2 ~ Beautiful Gift

Later on my husband and I wouldn't really remember verbatim what the deputies said to us—something about Brandon being at a friend's house and a gunshot wound believed to be self-inflicted. All I remember now about that moment is that they said my son did not survive the wound.

Surreal is the only word I can find to describe this moment. Even if someone had tried to explain to me what an event like this would feel like, they would have no way to convey it. No way to convey what it feels like when your heart shatters into thousands of pieces.

Mostly all I remember is asking Kenny, over and over, "What are we going to do? What are we going to do? What are we going to do?" That was the only thing I could say. Later I would come to understand that all mothers and fathers who have suffered the loss of a child have had the same experience and speak the same language of loss that I do.

The deputies asked if there was someone they could call for us. I couldn't think of anyone, couldn't make any decisions. I felt as if we were living someone else's nightmare. While I was talking to the deputies my husband called our neighbors Randy and Denise. They were in bed—it was 4:45 a.m.—and didn't pick up, but the phone call woke Denise. She saw that it was Kenny calling, looked out the window and saw cop cars parked in our driveway, woke up Randy, and they both came over. The deputies left when they arrived. One of the deputies had already called our priest. The priest was out of town, so Steve Witt, the deacon of our church, was on call. Steve drove to our house on icy roads and got there an hour after he received the call.

Kenny left for our twenty-three-year-old son Cody's apartment in Grinnell, twenty minutes away, to tell him the news—he didn't want Cody to hear it from some law enforcement officer that he didn't know. He also didn't want him driving on the icy road when he was so distraught.

Deacon Steve arrived after Kenny left. I sat at the kitchen table and Steve stood beside me. He prayed and I cried. "Tell me that he's safe in the arms of Jesus," I said desperately. "If you can tell me that I might be able to get through this. Otherwise I'll never get through it."

Steve reassured me that Brandon was in heaven, as he would keep reassuring me, along with the rest of my family, during the weeks and months to come.

He asked me if I wanted him to go to the house where Brandon was shot and bless his body. The deputies had told us that the incident happened at Brandon's friend's house, about three miles from where we lived.

"Yes, please," I said.

Steve left and came back forty-five minutes later, saying he hadn't been allowed to go into Brandon's friend's house and bless Brandon's body because the house was sealed off. Two Department of Criminal Investigation (DCI) officers were there and the house was considered a possible crime scene because two people had been present, Brandon and his friend Joshua, when the shooting took place. Steve said he had blessed the house instead.

Kenny tried calling our daughter Jessica to tell her about Brandon as he was driving back from Grinnell with Cody.

Jessica's only two years older than Brandon and they were very close. She was living in Scottsdale, Arizona – Brandon was going to move there the following week, he'd already gotten a job and he and Jessica had rented an apartment together.

Jessica and her boyfriend were staying at a friend's house. It was three-thirty in the morning in Arizona and they were both sound asleep. For some odd reason, Jessica woke up out of a sound sleep at four in the morning and decided to go home. Her phone battery was dead and she connected it to her car charger, then saw that she had four calls from her dad. The messages he'd left only said that she should call him back. She knew then that something was terribly wrong. She called Kenny back and he told her the news. She was so distraught she had to pull over and Johnny took over the driving.

Our phone started ringing and people started coming in droves: friends, neighbors, and family members. Kenny and I both come from big families—Kenny has five siblings and I'm the oldest of seven—and all of our brothers and sisters who live close by came immediately, and the ones who live farther away arrived within twenty-four hours. Kenny got back with Cody—even now I can hardly stand to think about how scared and distraught Cody was. He was pacing from room to room, cursing and asking *why*. Jessica's boyfriend Johnny got plane tickets for her and him and also for my mother, who lived in Arizona too; all three threw some clothes together, drove to the airport, and got here on the same day. Within a few hours of our hearing about Brandon, my best friend Debbie called from Alabama. She was crying so hard she could hardly talk. "I'll be there as soon as I can get there." She arrived late that night.

My house was taken over by my friends and family members. It was as if each person knew what their duties should be. Someone was in charge of answering telephone calls as the phone continued to ring. Others took turns accepting the food, drinks, and paper products new incoming guests were bringing. Others intercepted people who came to show respect and condolences, as I, Kenny, and Cody secluded ourselves in my bedroom to try to get our heads wrapped around the fact that Brandon had been taken from us. Reality would strike and there would be crying, moaning and weeping to the point where we all became exhausted. Then, I believe, our minds shut down again to protect us.

News filtered in all day about what was going on. The person who was with Brandon when he was shot, Brandon's friend Joshua, was a sheriff deputy reserve. It was his house and his gun, and there was some question about whether he had any involvement in Brandon's death. He told the authorities that he was asleep in bed and heard a gunshot that woke him up. He called the sheriff's department and told them that Brandon Smith had shot himself. He also told the authorities that earlier Brandon was cooking a hamburger. He said that Brandon was in and out of the kitchen, walking around the house, joking and talking on the phone, turning the bedroom lights on and off and laughing, and that Brandon had asked him several times to take him home. A few days later they made Joshua take a lie detector test while they interrogated him and he confirmed all of the above.

Kenny and I had to meet with one of the investigators at ten in the morning, nine hours after the shooting. They kept asking us whether Brandon was left handed or right handed and whether he ever talked about suicide. They told us they'd call us when the funeral home director picked up the body. We waited and waited. Finally at around twelve-thirty they called and said the body was being taken to the funeral home. Brandon's body had been lying on the floor for a total of almost twelve hours. None of us could imagine why the cops took so long to release it. Later we figured it had something to do with their investigation.

The next few days were filled with horror and shock. There was a two-day-long investigation by the Iowa Department of Criminal Investigation. The law enforcement officers were implying that Brandon had "completed" suicide. I told them that Brandon had never even picked up a handgun and he didn't know anything about handguns, as far as I knew. There, in the conference room at Kenny's office—we'd gone there to meet the investigator—Kenny and I looked at each other: What in the hell was going on?

Two years later I would hear a rumor that this same handgun, which Brandon was shot with had accidentally discharged, putting a hole in the ceiling at the sheriff's department. Then Joshua bought it and Brandon got shot with it. I was also told that it had a hair trigger and basically my son didn't stand a chance if he was handling it. Who knows in a small town how rumors get started, but this supposedly came from employees who worked in the sheriff's department and witnessed the gun going off. After I heard the rumor I ran into the person who owned this handgun before Joshua owned it – he sold the gun to Joshua because he'd gotten a new job and was moving to another town. I asked him if it was true that the gun went off when it was just being handled in the sheriff's department and he confirmed that episode had occurred.

Then there was the autopsy, the funeral arrangements, and the horrific things that had to be done to prepare the body. My friend Debbie had worked as an obstetrics nurse at the hospital where Brandon was born and was the first person to hold him on this earth. She felt as if he was one of her own children. I asked her to go and look at Brandon's body before I did, to make sure we could have an open casket viewing—something that haunts her to this day.

I brought Brandon's suit, shirt, tie, underwear, and socks to the funeral director so Brandon had clothes to be buried in. I don't even remember picking them out. I couldn't process what had happened. *They're going to make me put my son in a box in the ground?* I thought.

Despite this, I had to stay on task and try to function. I struggled to do what I had to do, and at the same time I kept thinking: *Who could be this cruel? God? The Devil? Who?* The anger I felt was beyond belief. I kept thinking, *No one can take one member of my family without taking the others. Or at least take me.* I couldn't believe I had to bury my child.

We had the funeral four days after Brandon died. By then the police investigation was pretty much over although they were still waiting for the toxicology report. They were testing Brandon's blood for drugs. I didn't hear more from the DCI department for two weeks and when I called the agent I spoke to said that the death had been ruled a "completed suicide."

"Really?" I said to the agent on the other end of the telephone line. "I think you've got it wrong. It was a foolish accident." There was a very long silence on his end of the telephone line.

That day our family became victims of suicide, as loved ones left behind are often referred to. I remember thinking, when the agent told me the conclusion was completed suicide, *something isn't right here*. I always pride myself on being very intuitive. I needed answers to questions. Did I miss something? Did Brandon have an undiagnosed mental illness? I oscillated back and forth between my feelings and searching for answers. I wanted some sort of epilogue to the story. My mind couldn't even comprehend life without Brandon. Thousands of scenarios were running through my head.

I decided to get the report and go through it myself, because of the unsettled feeling in my gut. The report came several weeks later. It was 233 pages long, and included the autopsy report, the results of the interrogation of Joshua, the results of the ballistic testing, interviews with various people, and a three-page document stating the DCI's conclusions. When it came I opened the envelope, glanced through a few pages, and put it away. I couldn't make myself look at it any more. Over the next few weeks and months I read through bits and pieces of it, but it was several years before I could go through the whole thing.

The report said the wound behind Brandon's right ear was the entrance wound. The doctor who wrote the autopsy report also said it was a contact wound, although there was no gunpowder found in Brandon's hair. I couldn't help thinking that the police had a stake in making it sound like Brandon had committed suicide because they were worried about liability regarding the gun: If the gun really was defective and had a hair trigger and they had sold it to someone and that's how it made its way into Brandon's hand on that horrible night in January 2008, his death could have reasonably been blamed on them.

The gun was found at Brandon's feet, which didn't make sense according to the suicide theory. My research told me that most of the time when there's a suicide the gun never leaves the hand of the person pulling the trigger because of what's referred to as cadaveric spasm. No fingerprints were found on the gun according to the DCI report, which I thought was also strange: Was it possible that Brandon never even touched the gun and it fell out of its case and went off? His hands were not bagged or protected in order to check for gunpowder residue and ensure that he in fact was the person that pulled the trigger.

The toxicology report showed no drugs in my son's body other than alcohol, not even marijuana. The report said that the investigators spoke to some people Brandon talked to in the bar the night he died and they all said he did not act distraught or depressed that night. Kenny and I also heard accounts from people who saw him that night and they all said he was just his normal self.

The DCI reported that according to Joshua there had been an altercation between him and Brandon earlier in the night, but Joshua said they patched it up on their own later on in the evening. Brandon's cell phone log showed he spoke to his cousin Marcus and wished him a happy birthday less than an hour before he died. Marcus said Brandon was laughing and happy when he talked to him on the phone.

I asked Joshua a few years after Brandon died if my son had ever mentioned intentionally harming himself and Joshua said no. I asked him if the magazine in the gun was loaded and he answered yes. I asked him if there was a safety on the gun and he answered no.

We were left with so many questions. But everyone in my family is certain that Brandon did not "complete" suicide. We have had to rise above what the death certificate said. Accidents that kill people are tragedies. Suicides are double tragedies. They involve feelings of guilt, shame and anger that seem to follow the survivors throughout their lives. We had something stolen from us that can never be replaced. Our hopes and dreams of Brandon's future, Brandon himself, were all gone. But what we feel is still different, I believe, than what we might feel if we believed he had intentionally shot himself.

We will never know exactly what took place on that fateful night. I have tried and tried to come up with the answer until I have almost driven myself to insanity. But whatever happened, it doesn't change the fact that my son is gone and not coming back to this world.

We cannot fix that—it is done. But we can choose how we're going to deal with this tragedy and go on. We've tried to honor Brandon's life and make this world a better place and make him proud.

And besides, as it turned out, Brandon's death was not the end of my beautiful boy or even of my relationship with him. It was just the beginning of the most important journey of my life, a journey toward healing and finding my son in the afterlife.

CHAPTER 2
THE DIMES

I believe my husband's sister, Cheryl, found the first dime. We were on our way to the funeral home for the visitation. There were twelve of us: Kenny and I, of course, and Kenny's parents and his sister Cheryl and her husband and my mother and my siblings and their partners and my two kids and my close friends Debbie and Kathy. We walked single file out the front door of my house and down the frozen snow-and ice-covered sidewalk. It was January in Iowa and we were having a terrible winter as far as ice, snow, and low temperatures.

Cheryl, Kenny's only sister, found a single dime lying on top of the icy snow on the sidewalk. "That's strange," she said.

In the car after the funeral she told us that a couple of months earlier she and the lady who owns the restaurant where she's a waitress were discussing the possibility of after-death communication when they were cleaning up at the end of the night, and the owner said she'd heard that people sometimes start finding coins after their loved ones pass. Strangely, I'd had a somewhat similar conversation myself a couple of weeks earlier than that. I was talking with a co-worker, Gwen, about life after death. As nurses, we'd both seen a lot of inexplicable things happening when people die, especially at the nursing home where I was the director when my kids were little and Gwen was the head night nurse—people seeing their dead loved ones right before they went and acting happy and peaceful to go with them, things like that.

The day Gwen and I had the conversation about coins as a means of communication from the afterlife, we were working together in the chemotherapy infusion center in a small town near where we both lived. Gwen told me that she had a friend who had lost her husband in a terrible tragedy. The friend had recently gone to see a medium speak to a crowd. During the talk, the medium singled out Gwen's friend and told her there was a strong sense of a loved one who had just passed, probably the spirit of her husband, around her. And then the spirit of Gwen's friend's husband asked her, through the medium, if she had been finding lots of dimes lately. She said that yes, she had—afterwards she told Gwen she'd been finding dimes in all sorts of strange places. The medium went on to tell her that her husband was saying he was using the dimes to try to get her attention, to let her know he was okay and communicate with her. That conversation with Gwen, three weeks before Brandon died, opened my mind to finding dimes as a way of after- death communication from loved ones.

Still, nobody thought much about that dime lying on the frozen sidewalk, the day we were leaving to go to the funeral home to view Brandon's body before the visitation. Although it caught Cheryl's eye gleaming in the frozen snow and she stopped to pick it up, we didn't pay much attention to it. Later she said that if she hadn't had that conversation at work she might not have even picked it up. And I didn't connect it with the conversation I'd had with Gwen until a few weeks later. We had no idea what would transpire in the next year or so.

Then Kenny and I started finding single dimes in the most peculiar places and at the most significant times. Single dimes turned up in the middle of my and Kenny's closet or on the floor in our bedroom—it would always be right in the middle of the floor so you couldn't miss it. Brandon's brother and sister also started finding dimes in their houses and cars, usually when they were having a hard time. Always just one single dime.

We all thought those dimes were strange and finally I said, "This has to be coming from Brandon." It was almost as if Brandon was saying, "Don't worry about me," or "Things are tough right now I know, but it's all going to be okay." But still I was a little skeptical. I believed in the afterlife, I felt Brandon was around us, but I wasn't completely convinced about the dimes.

Kenny was the first one in the family to start believing on a deeper level that Brandon really was around and trying to contact us. Until then Kenny hadn't thought much about the dimes—when I said, "This has to be coming from Brandon," he just looked at me skeptically—and when he started truly believing that Brandon was around it had to do with beer, not dimes.

It happened on Valentine's Day, about a month after Brandon died. Our friends David and Linda invited us for dinner and when we got to their house David said he had tried to buy a 24-pack of Bud Select for the dinner party but the store only had 18-packs so he bought one of those. When he was putting the beer in the refrigerator at home, the last two cans he took out of the box were Natural Light, not Bud Select. *How odd,* he thought. *That never happened before*. Linda looked at him and said, "That's the beer Brandon used to drink." He said they'd decided then and there that the beers must be a sign from Brandon—David has had experiences with ghosts of his own and they're both believers in the afterlife. But they had debated about whether to tell us because they thought it might upset us, and then they decided it was something we needed to know. After he told us the story David went to the refrigerator, took out the two cans of Natural Light—Natty Light, as Brandon used to call it – set them in front of us on the kitchen island and said, "I think these are for you."

Later on, when we got home, Kenny said he knew right away that those two cans of beer were telling us that Brandon was okay. Our son Cody was in Oregon on business that night. Kenny called him and told him the story and Cody said, "Well, you're not going to believe this, Dad, but the hotel I'm staying at has Natural Light on tap for a dollar a draw. I've never seen Natural Light on tap, ever."

That night when Kenny and I got into bed he said, "I really truly think that beer was a sign from Brandon." I'd never thought of Kenny as someone who was particularly open to signs from the afterlife, but sitting there next to him in bed I saw that he was.

We went to Arizona the day after the dinner with David and Linda, to pick up a car—Jessica's boyfriend Johnny was a car salesman and had bought the car for us at an auction—and drive it home. We needed the car and we felt like it might help us to go somewhere warm out of town. At the last minute Jessica and her Johnny decided to come back from Arizona with us to help with the driving. When we pulled into our driveway at the end of the trip, on Sunday night at around nine, Jessica and I looked down and noticed a single dime lying on the backseat between the two of us. We stared at each other, surprised.

One day in March I was having a particularly hard time. I couldn't stop crying and all I could focus on was wanting my son back. Finally I had to call Kenny at work and ask him to come home to try to help me. He came home, consoled me as best he could, and went back to work. He texted me the minute he got to his office. "I think Brandon's okay. I just found a dime in my shirt pocket."

I called him right away. "Really?" I said. "In your shirt pocket?" Anyone who knows Kenny knows that he is very well organized and regular in his habits. All he ever puts in his shirt pocket is his pen and pocket calculator. He never puts any kind of money or change there.

"I think Brandon's trying to give us a sign," he said. "I think he's trying to tell us he's just fine."

I realized that even though I'd been thinking of myself as the one in the family who believed in things like the afterlife, he was the one now who *really* believed, and now he was making me believe, that Brandon was reaching out to us.

I must say, finding the dimes did help me cope with the grief. Every time I thought I couldn't make it through, a dime would appear. Single dimes would just turn up in the car, on the driveway or on the sidewalk. Almost as if Brandon was saying, "Hey guys, listen to me, I'm fine!"

We were still devastated by the huge void in our lives.

I didn't want to do anything more than I had to; it was extremely hard to do even simple things like go to work or go to the grocery store or make dinner. I didn't want to leave my house, which was my refuge. I had gone back to work in February, but if I had to do it all over again I would take at least a year off. Emotional pain is exhausting physically. It's more tiring than doing hard physical labor for hours. That is something we learned early on in nurses' training. Debbie had to keep reminding me why I was so tired after Brandon died.

Kenny, Jessica, Cody, and I tried to keep our faith close and made it a point to be together as a family at least once a month. We had gone to a grief counselor right after Brandon passed. That helped but it was a long rough road and we knew we just had to walk down it together. We were pretty much shattered—physically, mentally and spiritually.

Brandon's car sat in our driveway for at least four months, and one day I decided to drive it somewhere. The car was an old jade-green Ford Taurus. It had a cassette tape deck in it, and as soon as I turned the key a song started playing: George Straight belting out I'm Carrying Your Love with Me: "I'll be moving with the good Lord's speed, carrying your love with me. It's my strength for holding on every minute that I have to be gone. I'll have everything I'll ever need, carrying your love with me." I sat in the car and had a good cry, but that song made me feel close to Brandon too. I felt like it was Brandon trying to send me another sign that he was okay. I noticed a dime sitting in the cup holder too. I drove his car to the grocery store that day, and I continued driving it all summer, until my mother moved back from Arizona at the end of August and I gave it to her because she didn't have a car.

My dear friend Debbie came to Iowa from where she lives in Alabama the day Brandon passed, stayed for ten days, and helped me pick up the pieces of my broken world. She ran the household, doing the dishes, coordinating rides for people going to and from the airport, sending my daughter out to buy me something to wear to the funeral. Before she went home she said she hoped I'd visit sometime soon, that we could rent a beach house for some relaxation since she's only an hour away from the Florida panhandle. I love the ocean and in April I flew to Fort Walton Beach, Florida, after a lot of coaxing from my friends. My friend Kathy and Debbie's daughter Ashley joined Debbie and me. We rented a house a block away from the beach. It was great to get away from the cold harsh weather we were having in Iowa. The white-sugar sand beaches and the smell and sound of the ocean brought a sense of peace to my soul.

One morning, while we were having coffee on the beach house porch, Kathy handed me a green cardboard box with a gold ribbon on it. I opened it, and inside, resting on some tissue, was a dark curly lock of hair – it was Brandon's hair, I could tell right away. Then I remembered that on the day of the visitation I had asked Kathy, who's a hairdresser, to go in and fix Brandon's hair, to put it back to the way he normally wore it. After the funeral my friend Rachael asked me if I had gotten a lock of hair. "No," I said, "I didn't even think about it at the time." Everything was so surreal at the time it was hard to even think or remember anything. But Kathy had thought of it. I thanked her and hugged her and we all had a good cry that morning on the porch. Then we packed up to go to the beach for some sun and rest.

Kathy loves the beach and likes to walk along picking up seashells, and within an hour she was picking up seashells down by the water's edge. After about forty-five minutes, she came running up to our spot on the beach holding out her hand with something in it. "Look what I found," she said. "I saw it wash up onto the shore with some seashells. Then a wave came and it got washed back out a little way, then another wave brought it back in and I grabbed it. What do you think it is? It's a coin, but is it a dime or a penny?" She handed the coin to me and I looked it over carefully. It was so corroded from the salt water it was hard to tell what it was, but I scraped a little of the corrosion off, and sure enough, it was a dime. That was the moment I became a believer, my first "ah ha" moment: *Maybe there is something to this dime thing*, I thought. *How could one dime wash up on the beach*? I supposed it could have fallen out of someone's pocket, but it looked like it had been in the ocean for quite a while.

I couldn't make out the date on it, so in August of that year I took it to a coin collector at the Iowa State Fair. He looked at it through a big magnifying glass and told me that the date on it was 1984. Kenny, Cody, Cody's girlfriend Britni, and I all looked at each other as if we had seen a ghost: 1984 is the year Cody was born. We walked around Pioneer Hall, discussing the coin and the date and what it all might mean. To me, it was Brandon's way of telling me I had work left to do in the world, that I still had Cody and Jessica to take care of, along with myself and Kenny and all the rest of my life.

Debbie asked me, that day at the beach, what the significance of the dime that came out of the ocean was – she could tell it meant something to me and she was intrigued. I told her that ever since Brandon had passed we had been finding single dimes and had been struggling to understand the meaning. It seemed like he was trying to communicate in some way.

At that point Debbie hadn't given much thought to the afterlife, let alone to the possibility of after-death communication through coins. Driving back to Alabama at end of the trip, after dropping off Kathy and me at separate airports, Debbie stopped at a random convenience store to grab a Diet Coke. She went to the counter to pay, looked down, and right there in the middle of the counter was a shiny dime. She gasped and left it lying on the counter. That was only the beginning of the dimes that Brandon was going to leave her. Soon she too would become a believer.

I was careful at first about who I shared my dime stories with. I knew most people would think I had lost my mind. Even I had been skeptical at first.

As time went on we noticed an increase in finding dimes. I would find them in the middle of the passenger side car seat, on the floor at work, in places where I had never seen dimes or any coins before—where there was no reason for there to be coins— like the tiny room at work where we mixed up the chemotherapy. They just seemed to turn up out of nowhere, usually when I, or someone in my family was feeling hopeless or unbearably sad about the loss of Brandon. (I've collected some of the more interesting dime stories in an appendix at the back of this book.)

The dimes were always shiny, not because they were new

but because they seemed to give off a little light of their own. It's as if Brandon wants to make sure we don't miss them. And, I believe, anything that comes from the other world has a little extra shine to it.

I had encouraged our daughter Jessica to continue going to therapy to help her through this devastating tragedy. She agreed to start seeing someone and made an appointment with a therapist a friend referred her to. On the day of her appointment, when she went to the desk to check in, there it was—a bright shining dime, sitting heads up on the counter. She took a picture of it and sent it to her dad and me. "Well, I think I was supposed to come here, according to Brandon," she wrote in the text.

The whole first year after Brandon passed was difficult, but I would have to say the holidays, birthdays, and anniversaries were absolutely the worst. It wasn't so much the day itself, but the anticipation of the day. Nothing seemed to matter much without Brandon. We tried to rely on God, each other, family, and close friends. Still, it was very difficult. My friend Debbie had a great idea for Brandon's birthday, June 10th. Debbie suggested getting balloons and launching them on Brandon's birthday. We gathered at the cemetery—Kenny and I along with six or eight of our closest friends. We let twenty-eight red, white, and blue balloons (it was Brandon's twenty-eighth birthday, red, white, and blue are the Chicago Cubs colors) fly up into the sky, some of them with dimes taped on cards; there were messages written on the cards too, we punched holes in the cards, threaded the balloon strings through the holes and tied knots in the ends. I remember standing there watching those balloons disappear into the sky, feeling a little bit better because we were celebrating Brandon's birthday, reaching out to him the way he'd been reaching out to us. Jessica, Cody, my mom, and some of Brandon's friends got together in Arizona that day too, had a barbecue with hotdogs and hamburgers, one of Brandon's favorite meals, and let some balloons go. My friend Debbie in Alabama let some balloons go, Brandon's cousins did it in New York City, and different people in several places in Iowa did the same thing.

When I arrived home from our celebration at the cemetery, there it was—one single dime sitting on top of a magazine on the arm of Kenny's recliner. It hadn't been there before we left.

I did some research on the Internet about people finding dimes or pennies that seemed to be sent from their dead loved ones. I found many accounts of people finding coins, particularly dimes or pennies, as signs from spirit. One website said coins showing up means your loved ones in spirit want you to know they're looking out for you, trying to get your attention, or offering validation that you're on the right path. Of course, we're still physical beings and our lost loved ones are now spiritual beings purely made of energy, so it seems odd that spiritual beings can sometimes use coins, which are definitely of the material world, as a means of communication. All I can say is that those dimes kept showing up. And that many people report on the Internet that the same thing has happened to them.

One by one, the people around us were starting to get the picture that dimes were one way Brandon would be communicating with the people he loved on this side. It seemed like Brandon was trying to convince the non-believers that in fact he was still here and they needed to know that.

One of the first times the Smith family got together for a holiday after Brandon's passing was over the 4th of July that year. Grandma Smith, Kenny's mother, had decided to have a picnic at her house and we were all invited. Kenny's parents still live on the farm where Kenny grew up, about five miles away from our house. They're in their early eighties but they still go places and do things and take an interest in everything. They have a busier activity schedule than I do—they never miss a play or a church confirmation or a football game one of their grandchildren is taking part in.

That 4th of July, Grandma Smith had decided to grill outside and have the barbecue in the machine shed on the farm. Grandpa had spent a lot of time cleaning the machine shed, moving out the tractors and equipment and sweeping the floor. On the morning of the 4th Grandma asked Grandpa to please help her move a card table into the shed.

She had been working on some family history and ancestry things and all the print-outs were sitting in a stack on the card table. When it was almost time for us to arrive, Grandpa went in the house to move the table. Grandma picked up her family history papers, and there lying in the middle of the table was a single shiny dime. I guess we were not going to have a picnic without Brandon letting us know he was there.

As soon as we arrived Grandpa looked hard at Grandma and said, "Mom, tell them what you found."

Grandma told us about how she had asked Grandpa to move the table for her. "Look at what I found under the papers on it," she said, pointing at the dime sitting in the middle on the counter. For the last few weeks we had been talking to Grandma and Grandpa about how we had been finding dimes and what we thought it meant. They hadn't said much when we talked about it and we figured that they were probably, understandably, a little skeptical. Now both their faces were filled with wonder, confusion, and surprise. "Oh my goodness, how did that get under there?" Grandma said over and over. I think that was when Kenny's parents started believing in the dimes.

Grandpa and Grandma volunteer at the Iowa State Fair every year. They usually camp in the campground inside the fairgrounds for the week and volunteer in the information booth or give people rides in a golf cart from point A to point B. They look forward to the fair all year. During the week of the fair they always go to the mass offered on Sunday mornings at Pioneer Hall, located at the top of a hill in the fairgrounds. Pioneer Hall has lots of antiques, old machinery, and pottery on display as well as concession stands and country and gospel music acts performing throughout the week.

Grandma and Grandpa went to mass in Pioneer Hall on Sunday morning, the year of Brandon's death. They picked a random seat. After they sat down, Grandpa looked down and saw a single shiny dime lying on the floor between his feet.

My younger brother Mark was devastated by Brandon's death, like all of us were. Mark lives three miles away from us. He's about ten years older than Brandon. Mark was one of Brandon's best friends and Brandon always looked up to him. They hung out together a lot, golfing, boating, eating steaks in the clubhouse, going to the American Legion for catfish dinners. They were both jokesters; they loved to tease me about everything, even the pictures on my walls, throwing back their heads and laughing together with the pleasure of it. Mark was so shattered after Brandon died it took him weeks to let it sink in, but he tried his best to help us and hold us together, doing some of the things Brandon used to do—little things like helping Kenny get the pontoon out.

One Friday night, about five months after Brandon passed Mark called me at around nine o'clock. He said that earlier that day he was at Brandon's grave and wiped down the headstone. After he was finished he walked to his truck, and sitting on the seat was a dime. He didn't think much about it; he figured it could've fallen out of his pocket. Then he drove to the country club to play golf. He glanced at the seat of his truck before he got out—there was nothing on it. After golfing and eating a steak he returned to his pickup, opened the door, and saw, once again, lying on the driver's seat, a single dime. "I thought it was really strange," he said, during our phone call.

I told him it was just Brandon saying, "Thanks for cleaning off my headstone."

"But that wasn't the weirdest thing that happened," he said. "When I got home I opened my billfold to see how much money I'd spent, and there was a dime. How in the world did a dime get into my billfold? I don't even have a place for change in my billfold." He was so freaked out he was almost crying.

I told him I had no idea how that dime got into his billfold. Some things you just can't explain. "Don't worry," I said. "That was just Brandon's way of communicating with you." I'm not sure I ever convinced Mark of that. To this day he can't understand why there was a single dime sitting in the crease of his billfold. And he continues to find dimes.

My husband's younger brother David and Brandon were also close. Kenny, David, and their older brother Mike used to own a condo together at the Lake of the Ozarks, and over the years our families spent a considerable amount of time together boating, swimming, and trying out all the new restaurants on the lake. When Brandon and Cody were both in their early and mid-twenties their Uncle David offered to chaperone them in the evenings to all the newest happening spots on the lake. That's probably when they came up with the nickname Uncle Buck for David, after the old John Candy comedy about an uncle who babysits his brother's rebellious children.

David called his brother Kenny every day for at least five years after Brandon passed. He wanted to be there for him during this difficult time. During the first year after Brandon passed, David was sure that this dime thing was just something Kenny and I believed in. He himself wasn't convinced, but he wanted nothing more than to let us believe whatever helped us along the way. He listened to our stories about the dimes, never saying a word. Then one summer afternoon, while we were sitting on my deck with David and his wife Pam he listened to us discuss after-death communication, David said that he really didn't believe in all that. Not that he didn't believe in the afterlife he just didn't think dead people could communicate.

Then one night David stopped at a store to pick up some

Chex-mix for his children on his way to Lake of the Ozarks; his kids, Sawyer and Kennedy, in their early teens, were joining him at the lake for a weekend. I got a call from him at about nine in the evening. He sounded excited and a little scared.

"I was just walking to my car in the parking lot and it was like this dime just came out of nowhere," he said. "It hit the pavement and landed right in front of my foot. I heard the noise of the dime hitting the pavement. I only had a money clip with bills in it. I had on mesh shorts with no pockets and a t-shirt with no pocket. I didn't have any coins on me at all. It's like that dime dropped out of the sky and landed right in front of my face. I looked up and said, 'Okay, Brandon, I believe!'"

"That's what I've been trying to tell you, David. Brandon's letting you know he's still with us. Plus I'm sure he's getting a big kick out of trying to convince you, because you were a non-believer."

"Well, I'm convinced now," he said. "I have no idea where that dime came from!" He also said that when he was driving, right before he stopped at the store for the Chex-mix, he heard a song on the radio that my friend's daughter sang at Brandon's funeral, *I Can Only Imagine,* and right before the song came on he was thinking about all the times Brandon had driven to the Lake of the Ozarks with him, remembering some of the things they had talked about during the five-and-half-hour drive.

"Now you can be part of our little group of believers," I said, and David started laughing.

Brandon was very persistent in making believers out of us all.

CHAPTER 3

THE DREAMS

Many people have contact with their deceased loved ones in dreams. Dreams are certainly a more common way of after-death communication than dimes.

Some of us have had dreams about Brandon too. I would have to wait seven and a half years to have a dream about him myself. But when I lost my dad, more than thirty years ago, I had a vivid dream the day before his funeral in which he came to me. At the end of the dream he went to a door and I saw that beyond that door was a long hallway filled with the brightest light I'd ever seen. I was twenty-three when I had that dream and a few weeks pregnant with Brandon, though I didn't know it at the time. Now, when I look back, I feel like that's why my father came to me—he wanted to reassure me that he was okay so his death wouldn't add stress to my pregnancy. My father was fifty-one when he died, and when I lost Brandon I was fifty-one, and I've always felt that my father's death and Brandon's birth and even Brandon's death were linked in some way. The dream I had about my father paved the way for my searching and finding Brandon in the afterlife, because it gave me a solid belief in the afterlife.

∾

During September of 2008, around eight months after Brandon passed, Grandpa Smith came up to me after church one Sunday and said, "Lesa, I want to tell you about this dream I had of Brandon. I'll try real hard not to cry."

Brandon and Grandpa Smith had a special relationship. They were both talkers; they both loved to tell stories and tell their stories to each other. Grandpa always said that when Brandon walked into a room the room would light up, and whenever Brandon was around Grandpa always had an extra twinkle in his eyes.

In the September before Brandon died, all of the males in Kenny's family—Kenny and his brothers and their sons and our two sons—got together to put a roof on Grandma and Grandpa's house. Grandpa put Brandon in charge and Brandon felt really pleased that his grandfather had so much faith in him. The roof was finished in two days and when it was done Grandpa stood outside the house and looked up at the new roof with a big smile on his face. He clapped Brandon on the shoulder and said, "Well done!"

Grandpa Smith still misses Brandon terribly. I don't think I've seen the same happy smile on his face that he used to have most of the time, since Brandon died.

Grandpa Smith was scheduled for surgery to have a pacemaker defibrillator attached to his heart when he approached me after church that day in September of the year Brandon died.

He wasn't convinced that he needed the pacemaker and he was apprehensive about the surgery and unsure about whether to go through with it. His heart was showing signs of going into a very dangerous rhythm and the doctors were adamant that he had to have it.

"It was so real," Grandpa said now, about the dream. "I think Brandon came to me. I was dreaming that I was standing in a pew here, in this church, and there were people standing around me, talking and laughing, like they were making fun of me. I started getting angry and turned to leave the church. Then I saw Brandon standing beside me in the pew. He put his arm around me. [Brandon always put his arm around his grandpa when he was with him here on earth]. He looked at me and smiled and said, "Grandpa, go ahead and have the surgery. You'll come through it fine, everything is going to be fine. Please don't worry about having the operation."

To this day Grandpa swears Brandon was standing at his bedside that night. I believe him. The surgery was a success and has saved Grandpa's life. He tells me he had never experienced such a vivid dream before—it seemed so real to him. I'm sure it was real, that it was Brandon reassuring his grandfather. Never failing to take care of those he loves.

Brandon has given some of his close friends important messages in vivid dreams too. Brandon's friend Miranda grew up near us and she and Brandon were fast friends for most of their lives— they rode bikes together, were partners in crime together; when they were four they disappeared up the gravel road, following our dog Pickles, and we didn't find them for at least half an hour.

Miranda has brown eyes and long straight dark hair; she and Brandon always looked alike—people always thought they were twins—and they'd probably still resemble each other if Brandon was here in a body. These days Miranda lives in Pella, forty-five minutes away from us, with her husband and three children. Miranda's second child, Trinity, was born in February 2008, a month after Brandon died. She was born with Spina bifida, a birth defect that happens when a baby's spine doesn't form normally, potentially damaging the nerves in the spinal cord. As a result Trinity has had to face more adversities in her seven-year life than most people do in a lifetime; she's had to have thirty-plus surgeries, several of which have been life threatening.

The night before her first surgery Brandon came to Miranda, who was understandably very upset, in a dream. In the dream he sat across from her at a table and told her it would be all right. Later she told her mother that it was so real it was as if he was there. She *knew* it was him—there was no doubt. Ever since, before almost every one of Trinity's serious surgical procedures, Miranda has found a dime or Brandon has come to her in a dream, reassuring her once again that everything will be all right. And so far it always has been.

A year or so after Brandon's death he came to Miranda with a message, not for her but for us, in one of the many vivid dreams she's had of him. At the time Kenny and I were planning to sell our house. We had been looking at other places and had put our house on the market. We live in a house on Lake Ponderosa, a small man-made lake surrounded by oak and hickory trees. When I was fourteen my parents bought a house on the lake and we moved into it full time. Kenny's parents had a small vacation cabin there too and he and I met a few weeks after I moved to the lake. We got married when we were eighteen and nineteen respectively and lived for a while in his parents' cabin before we moved to the country and tried our hands at farming (and Kenny's parents sold their cabin on the lake). When our youngest, Cody, went to college we sold our acreage and bought a two-story, four-bedroom house on the lake. The house is right on the water, surrounded by trees. Brandon helped us build our deck and remodel parts of the inside of the house.

One day, during the summer before he died, something funny happened that I couldn't stop thinking about after he died. He had been out on the lake in our pontoon with a friend the night before and had somehow accidentally dropped his wallet, a billfold with a metal money clip, in the water by the dock. There was money in it plus his license and his debit card and everything else you put in a wallet. That day when I came home from work and looked out at the lake, I saw Brandon standing in the water up to his chin, his head tilted back and his hair standing on end like Kramer's hair on Seinfeld.

Brandon had grown his hair out and it was sticking up because it had been mashed down all day under his baseball hat while he worked at his construction job. The job was only temporary while he figured out what else he wanted to do. Kenny has a twenty-five-year-old insurance business, and Brandon had worked hard all year to get five different licenses to sell insurance with Kenny. But it turned out that sitting in an office selling insurance wasn't Brandon's cup of tea—he didn't like it at all.

I like to think that if he had lived he would have ended up being an actor or a writer or doing something else that used his true talents.

That day, standing in the water up to his chin, he had a pole in one hand—later he told me the pole had a hockey-puck-size magnet attached to it, he had borrowed the magnet from work—and a rake in the other hand and he was fishing around with both of them in the water.

"What are you *doing*?" I screamed at him from the deck.

He yelled back the story of losing his billfold when they were coming in to dock the pontoon. "I know just where I dropped it!"

"You're never going to find that," I said.

All of a sudden he stopped, then disappeared under the water. He stayed under for about thirty seconds and emerged with a big victorious grin on his face. He raised his arm in the air, clutching the dripping black billfold, and yelled, "I found it!"

Later, when he was back in dry clothes and we were both sitting at the kitchen table, he looked at me, grinned, and said, "Don't tell Dad I dropped my wallet in the water. He'll think I'm an idiot."

Everything about this house reminded us of Brandon after he died. He had lived with us here for a while after college, he had helped us remodel, and the house was full of daily reminders that were painful. Kenny and I thought that maybe if we didn't have to see these reminders every day, it would somehow make it easier to live without Brandon.

In the dream Brandon said to Miranda, "You've got to get

a message to my mom and dad. Please tell them not to sell the house, please tell them." Miranda said he wasn't going to give up until she promised to relay the message to us. When she told us about the dream I thought, *That's weird, but there must be a reason why Brandon wants us to stay put.* I know my son well enough to know he was not going to stop until we paid attention to that message, no matter what. We discontinued our search for a new house. Looking back, I'm very happy we held onto our beautiful house by the lake, and I know now that selling it wouldn't have made the pain of losing Brandon go away.

∾

Brandon's childhood friend Alexa had an interesting dream about Brandon too, one that came with a message that by then I had heard several times before. In 2013, around the anniversary of Brandon's death, Alexa called her mom early one morning crying. "I spoke with Brandon last night in a dream," she said. "He was kneeling beside my bed. You need to call Lesa and tell her what he said, Mom. He wants her to know."

Recently I asked Alexa to tell me again what Brandon said to her in the dream, and here's what she told me. "It wasn't a long conversation. It was short, sweet, and to the point. I remember waking up and wanting to go back to that dream so bad. It was bright and he was wearing a white t-shirt. I hugged him and he gave me the biggest hug back. Kind of like the one he gave me the last time I saw him on the night before Thanksgiving. I told him how everyone missed him and especially his family.

He said, 'I know, but I'm ok, I'm ok.' I said to him, 'I just don't understand what happened.' I was talking about how he got shot, whether he shot himself. He looked at me and put his hand on my shoulder and said these exact words, "Come on, you know me, I would never do that.' It was at that exact moment I woke up from the dream. There were tears streaming down my face."

Alexa went on to say, "I often catch myself wondering why he chose to come to me. To this day I'm not sure, but I'm so glad he did because I know that he's okay."

On August 3, 2015, the night before a phone date with Jamie Butler, the psychic medium I'd been meeting with regularly for almost six years by then, I finally had a dream about Brandon myself. Brandon had been coming through loud and clear in those meetings with Jamie, and during every meeting I begged him to come to me in a dream—I wanted to see his face. I'd stare and stare at his face in pictures, trying to engrave it on my memory, sad because I'd never see it again until I was in the afterlife myself. And I kept saying to him in our meetings, "Why can't I have a dream about you?"

He said I wasn't ready, that he'd come to me in a dream when I was done with grieving, that having a dream about him before that would just make me sadder. He also said, "I'm real. I don't want you to think I'm not available to you except only in some sleep state." And then he added with his typical wise-guy sense of humor, "You're not Snow White or Sleeping Beauty." Besides, he said, he wanted to communicate with me when I was in "awake state" so he could get his message across more clearly.

But then, finally, on that August night in 2015, after seven and a half years of not dreaming about him, I did see him in a dream. In the dream he was exactly the same age he was when he passed—twenty-seven—and he looked exactly the same, with dark curly hair and bright hazel eyes and that beautiful grin of his. We went shopping together, as we often did. (That was one my favorite things about Brandon—he would shop with me for hours, whereas his brother Cody and my husband Kenny only last for about fifteen minutes; after Brandon died it was years before I could go near a men's clothing store.) In the dream, Brandon and I bought a new pair of blue jeans, two shirts (one with the Cubs baseball emblem on it), and a new pair of tennis shoes—all for him, just like in real life. He had plans to go to an '80s big-hair-band concert and everything seemed so normal between us. He was very much alive and well, looking great in his new clothes, which he put on right away. We were laughing together and having the same conversations we always had when he was here with me. When I woke up I had a smile on my face, and I couldn't stop smiling all morning.

CHAPTER 4

JAMIE

After Brandon died I knew right away that I wanted to find a clairvoyant—someone whose special gifts allow them to see and hear and pass on communications from spirits. There was a lot of stuff in the media at the time about after-death communication and I knew I wanted to try to reach Brandon, but I also knew I had to be extremely careful to find a clairvoyant who had a true gift. I looked for almost a year but couldn't find anybody I wanted to try. My grief was probably too fresh for me to be ready for that anyway.

Then in November of 2009, almost a year after Brandon's death, Jessica told me she'd just found out that a close friend of hers had been talking to his parents through a medium for the past six years; he told Jessica that she was the real deal. It was on January 6th, 2009, four days before the one-year anniversary of Brandon's passing, that I first made contact with my son through Jamie.

She started our phone call by telling me that Brandon was there with her. She described his appearance by saying he looked vibrant and young with dark curly hair and a beautiful smile. This described him perfectly—whenever Brandon walked into a room the place would light up. Jamie went on to say he was physically fit and had no mustache. She also described the way Brandon was sitting – leaning forward with his forearms on both knees, his hands clasped. That is exactly how he used to sit. It caught my attention right away and so did the incredibly accurate description of his physical appearance.

She said there were two spirits there with him that day. "One's a male and one's a female." Then she went on to say that one of them was Brandon's maternal grandfather, my father; he'd come to me in that dream shortly after he died and it made sense that he'd come to speak to me through Jamie now. "The female spirit here," Jamie said, "is your paternal grandmother." This, I knew, was my father's mother, my grandmother, Henrietta. This did surprise me—Henrietta passed in 1946, ten years before I was born. In a little while I'd find out there was a reason for her to be here today.

Then my conversation with Brandon, through Jamie, began.

I was uncertain how this whole thing worked, so Jamie explained that I could ask Brandon questions and he'd give his reply through her and that sometimes he'd have his own messages he wanted her to relay to us. "I can hear him and see him and the spirits who are with him," she said.

I asked her to ask Brandon if he was okay. This was my first time talking to her or any clairvoyant and I had no idea how the conversation would go. I had tons of questions I didn't really know how to ask. And I felt extremely emotional—I cried more on this day, during the appointment with Jamie, than I had since Brandon's funeral. But I hadn't started crying yet—I was still trying to get my bearings. Brandon's reply to my first question, conveyed by Jamie, was, "Yes, Mom, I'm fine. I'm so happy you're open to this kind of communication with me."

Then Jamie said something that floored me. "I see a gun and it firing, causing his death."

"Yes," I said and started to cry. "He was killed by a huge .40-caliber handgun with no safety, something cops carry around. I can't imagine what the hell something like that would have been doing lying around where Brandon was that night or how he could have gotten shot with it. My son knew nothing about handguns. I don't think he'd even ever had one in his hands. The department of criminal investigation investigated and ruled that his death was a completed suicide. I just don't know what to think and it's driving me to the brink of insanity.

"Brandon, what happened?" I asked desperately.

Jamie described to me what she saw: Brandon getting down on his knees as if he was pleading or begging. "I'm so sorry, Mom, please forgive me," she said he said. "It was a foolish accident and not intentional. You have to know that." Jamie told me that Brandon said, "I would never do that to you or my family. But most of all, I would never do that to myself."

I started crying so hard I could hardly breathe. I was relieved to hear Brandon confirm what I already knew in my heart—that he would never have killed himself—but I had been questioning it and second-guessing myself, wondering all sorts of things: Had I missed something? Had Brandon been depressed or mentally ill and I just hadn't accepted it? Despite what I'd heard just now from him, I felt like I needed to put those worries to rest and I asked Jamie to ask him if he was depressed.

He seemed a little irritated that I would even ask that question. His reply was, "*No*, about what? What did I have to be depressed about, Mom?" Jamie told me that she could usually tell if someone had a problem with depression or other mental health issues when they were on earth, and she didn't get that impression from Brandon at all. She went on to describe him as being very remorseful and said he wanted to let me know beyond a shadow of a doubt that he'd never had any intention of taking his life. He also relayed the message through Jamie that he felt very foolish and ashamed about what happened to cause his death.

He described how he was fooling around and heard a loud pop that scared him and he threw the gun down. Which now makes complete sense; the gun was found at his feet, according to the DCI report. He said that he found himself standing beside his body. He tried desperately to get back inside his body and he couldn't. Then he realized that he had died.

Hearing Brandon describe trying so hard to get back into his body, to not leave this earth, made me feel sick to my stomach, but it was also a relief. He really did not do this on purpose, I thought. It *was* a stupid accident, just as I had known in my heart all along. I had been second-guessing myself instead of listening to my gut instinct, but now I knew my gut instinct had been right and that it's always right, especially when it comes to my children. No one knows a child, even an adult child, better than a mother.

After a few moments, when I took all of that in, I asked Bandon who was there to meet him and take him to the other side. I asked him if my father came to get him when he crossed over. "No," he said. He said that once he figured out he wasn't going to get back in his body, he turned around and a lady was standing there waiting for him and he asked, 'Who are you?'

"Mom, it was great grandma, Grandma Henrietta," he said through Jamie. "She came to get me when I passed and now I can't get rid of her. She follows me everywhere!"

"Good!" I said. Brandon, of course, had never met his great grandmother, who died in 1946, and I'm pretty sure he had never even seen a picture of her. Now he seemed a little annoyed by her constant supervision.

Henrietta had a message for me too—she asked Jamie to pass this on to me: "When you hear the birds singing, think of me, because that's me." Jamie commented that Henrietta was hard to understand because she spoke with a heavy accent. I started smiling because I knew why she was hard to understand – my father's parents came from Holland with my dad's oldest brother and sister, arrived at Ellis Island and eventually settled in a small town in Iowa. They never spoke anything but Dutch at home and spoke just enough broken English to get by out in the world. There was no possible way Jamie could have known these things, and what she said about Henrietta's accent convinced me that she was legitimate even more than I was already convinced.

Brandon went on to talk about what dying is like. I didn't ask him about his death and if it was painful but the question was in my mind and it was almost as if he was reading my mind, then answering my questions. "Mom," he began. "Dying is like being born. It doesn't hurt. You feel like you're in a warm pool of water, just floating. No pain. So don't be afraid of death. Don't worry, Mom, I'll be here to catch you when you fall."

Tears came flooding down my face. "I know you will, sweetheart," I said, "and I'll look forward to the time when I get to see your beautiful face again." I meant it too. In that moment I stopped being afraid of death and started looking at death in a completely different way, and I've never lost that view. I see now that death is just another natural part of life, like birth is, and that the way most people look at death, the way I used to see it myself—as something horrible, to be feared and dreaded—is just a false story. It was a huge relief to me to hear, during this first meeting with Jamie, that Brandon hadn't suffered when he died and that he was happy and okay. And in the long run, coming to see that death isn't something to dread or worry about has been an enormous gift, like having a load lifted off my soul and my shoulders.

"What are you doing there, where you are?" I asked Brandon.

Jamie told me he got very excited and said, "Mom, I'm learning so much here! I'm learning without books!" Brandon asked Jamie to relay to me a story he'd learned, about a rug maker who noticed that as carefully as he tried to design rugs, they still had imperfections, and he realized that life is not perfect, but yet we can still strive to see the beauty in it.

I believe he told me that story because he wanted me to know that life isn't perfect and there was nothing I could have done to prevent what happened to him. He was trying to make me go on with my life and be grateful for what I did have. I was still in a very dark place—Brandon had only been dead for a year – and crawling back up to real life was going to be a process and a long journey and that's normal, even inevitable, for anyone who's experienced the loss I had experienced. But I appreciated Brandon's message.

Then Brandon told me, through Jamie, that I was the strongest one in my family in terms of trying to keep the family together—that is, with him still being part of it—and he was very happy I was doing that.

"Tell Dad I hear him when he talks to me in the car," Brandon said through Jamie. I didn't know Kenny was doing that. When I told Kenny what Jamie had passed along from Brandon he started crying and said, "I always talk to him when I'm alone driving by myself in the car."

I had been struggling with what a pamphlet I'd read, given to me by Compassionate Friends, called complicated grief. The pamphlet said that parental grief is intense, long lasting and complex, and that some people—not the grieving family but people looking at the situation from the outside—believe that when the child was an adult the pain of losing them is less. If the adult child's death involved alcohol or self-inflicted gun wounds or something else with social stigma attached to it, like Brandon's did, people can sometimes act judgmental, saying things that imply the adult child died as the result of his own bad choices and using that as a reason to dismiss the family's grief. This, the pamphlet said, adds to the parents' intense pain by creating in them a sense of isolation and defeat. Which in fact is what I was feeling at that time.

Today, during the meeting with Jamie and Brandon, Brandon told me not to worry about what anyone else says or thinks about anything, including what I was doing right now, because it really doesn't matter what other people think. I believe he was trying to spare us unnecessary pain and suffering. I think he also wanted to make sure we weren't blaming ourselves for what happened to him or taking to heart any judgmental statements anyone made.

A few years later, after I had been talking to Brandon through Jamie regularly for a while, the subject of the police ruling Brandon's death a suicide came up again. "[What happened to me] was a one in a million accident," Brandon said. "When you come across those, people don't understand them, so they tend to label them as suicide or something done on purpose, because that sounds more logical than a freak accident. That's really hard really hard for the loved ones left behind – having it be an accident and be labeled something else."

When I repeated that we had risen above that and didn't really care any more what the death certificate said, Brandon said, "That's so important." ("Wow, he's getting really loud," Jamie added). "Because there are thousands, Mom, thousands of cases where this has happened and the police and people around you label it as a suicide. Then these people have a story out there in the public eye that only partly resembles what the real story was. Because of the mislabeling of a death."

Brandon went on to describe how he came to be handling the gun that killed him. "Someone like me who touches everything and not being scared to touch anything," he said. "I can't count the number of times you told me not to touch things [when I was a kid]. But I always touched things anyway, including that gun. I was just horsing around, touching everything, it was so stupid. It was stupid, but that's my personality."

Jamie said he got really quiet after that.

In the next part of the conversation, during that first meeting with Jamie, I told Brandon that a group of our friends went to his house after he passed and cleaned and packed his things so we wouldn't have to do it. I couldn't bear to go through his clothes and the boxes of his things that our friends brought to our house   .

"They're just things, Mom," Brandon said through Jamie. "I have no attachment to material things. I hope that someday you'll be able to look back at something that reminds you of me and smile." I thought to myself that that day would never come. It took a few years, but once again he proved me wrong. These days, when I see something like a box of his old baseball cards in the basement, the words "Mixture of Good Cards" written on top in his handwriting with a black sharpie pen, I smile and remember how he used to think his baseball card collection was going to make him wealthy someday.

The hour was going by so quickly and I had so many more questions for him. I asked him if he was with me at the house. It was almost as if I'd see a shadow out of my peripheral vision and then when I turned the shadow would be gone. Some night I'm going to get up in the night, walk down the hall to the kitchen and find him standing at the breakfast bar, I thought.

"I'm always with you, Mom, only on a different plane," he told me. "It's kind of like coming in through a different door, but I'm right here beside you every day. Also, Mom, quit telling people you lost your son. You haven't lost me at all!" This made me laugh and cry at the same time. It was so much something Brandon would say and how he would say it. "And one more thing, Mom. Please quit looking up into the sky and talking to me, because I'm right here beside you. I've never left your side! I'll always be here with you."

I started firing questions at Brandon as fast as I could. "What about the dimes we've been finding?" I asked. "Are those coming from you?"

"Yes, Mom, that is me! I'm trying to let you know I'm still with you and I'm just fine."

"Why dimes?" I asked.

"I really didn't think pennies were enough," he said. "I thought you were worth more than that, so I decided to leave the dimes." In a later meeting with Jamie Brandon would tell me more about the dimes and how he managed to send them.

When the dimes were mentioned Jamie said, "Why do I see Florida? Don't you live in Arizona?"

I said, "I live in Iowa and am just visiting my daughter and son in Arizona now. But in April I was in Florida and I found a dime that washed up on the shore from the ocean." I thought of how finding that sea-water-corroded dime had been an ah ha moment for me, especially when I saw that Cody's year of birth was the date on it. Jamie mentioning Florida in connection to the dimes was another confirmation for me that she was the real deal and that the messages she was passing on to me really came from Brandon.

That first telephone conversation with Jamie ended up lasting for over an hour. I told Brandon I was keeping a journal about the dimes our close friends and family members were finding, and that the dimes made us all feel better. I said I was contemplating writing a book about his after-death communication with us, to help people know there's life on the other side and that your loved ones never really leave you.

Brandon said, "Oh, you should write a book, Mom! And I have the perfect name for it."

"What's that?"

"How I Found My Son."

When I hung up from Jamie I was exhausted but overcome with happiness. I went inside Jessica's apartment—I'd gone outside and sat in her car during the phone call—and told Jessica, Cody, and Cody's girlfriend Britni about the whole conversation with Brandon.

"Wow, we finally have our mom back," Cody said at one point during the retelling.

I knew it was true. The relief I felt was enormous. Not only did I know that Brandon was still around somewhere, not only had I just talked to him and knew that I would talk to him again, but what he said about how he died had given me tremendous relief.

When I told Cody and Jessica what Brandon communicated about his death being an accident and definitely not a suicide, Cody said, "Mom, you know if he was going to take his own life he would have written us a five-chapter book as to why he'd decided to do it. He might still not be finished with it!"

We all laughed at this because we knew it was true. For the first time in almost a year we felt some happiness and relief, because now we knew that the Brandon we all loved and cared about so much was still with us, still part of our family. Even though there were some tears, I remember the smiles on our faces and the hope in our hearts when I think of that moment.

And that was just the beginning of our new relationship with Brandon.

Chapter 5

Atlanta

In July 2009 I decided to travel to Atlanta to have my second meeting with Jamie in person. I wanted to meet face-to-face with this person who was helping me communicate with Brandon.

My friend Kathy and I made the trip from Iowa by car. It took us two days and when we got to Atlanta we found our hotel and spent the night. The next morning we drove to Jamie's studio and got there fifteen minutes early. Jamie pulled up in a small silver car, got out, and introduced herself to us with a friendly smile. She was a small attractive woman in her thirties, with blond hair and piercing beautiful blue eyes—the most beautiful eyes I've ever seen. I felt, standing there on the front walk looking at her, like I could somehow see into her eyes and through them to something beyond her, a feeling I continued to have as the meeting went on. Once we got inside the studio—a simple room with two modern couches, a coffee table, and two chairs, with very high ceilings and a loft—Jamie said Brandon had come to her the night before and told her she'd better get there early today, because his mom would be there fifteen minutes early. She said he was very excited and told her he had lots of things to tell me. "Boy, he is relentless!" Jamie said.

"That's Brandon," I said. I was already feeling better than I had since the last meeting with Jamie.

On the way to Atlanta Kathy and I had discussed a number of issues that were of concern to me. I was having a pity party for myself about my disappointment that Brandon was never going to get married, have children, and enjoy life growing with his family. When I look back on it now I see that these were my dreams for Brandon and that they might not have been his dreams. But when we made that trip to Georgia it was only a year and a half after Brandon's death and I was still pretty heavy in my grief. He had such a short time on this earth, I thought, how unfair. Kathy and I continued talking about all this as we drove, not knowing Brandon would address these very issues with me, through Jamie, when I got to Atlanta, as if he knew what was on my mind.

We got settled in Jamie's studio—I sat on one couch and my friend Kathy sat on the other and Jamie sat across from me. Jamie asked me if I wanted her to write down what we said today and I told her I had brought my own tape recorder. We set up the tape recorder and turned it on, and then I asked Jamie who was there with Brandon. Jamie said it was my father; his mother, my grandmother, Henrietta; and my maternal great-grandfather John Ross, who died when I was two, in 1958.

Jamie got quiet and appeared to listen for a minute, smiling and shaking her head. "Did Brandon always talk and never shut up?" she asked me laughing.

"Yes," I said, "he liked to talk a lot."

"Wow, how did you handle that?" Jamie said. She turned her head as if speaking to Brandon. "What are you saying?" she asked.

"Nothin'," Jamie said Brandon's reply was.

Jamie explained that Brandon had positioned himself next to me on the couch. "He's sitting on the edge of the couch with his feet over here," she pointed to the arm of the couch next to me. "He's not standing anymore, he's very casual."

Jamie described what Brandon looked like. "His hair is cut short. It's nice and thick, not thin." She commented on the fact that Brandon had dark hair instead of blond hair like I do and I told her that his hair is like my father's. "Beautiful dark brown and curly."

She said he was sitting beside me with one arm behind me, kind of around to the side, like he was leaning over me. "It looks like an Olin Mills picture; you know how they make you pose. There you go—you can put your hand right in him. You should be able to feel a difference. It will be either hot or cold, or a tingle or feel like tension, some kind of difference. He said he's okay with that. He's saying you were a snuggler and hugged and squeezed him a lot when he was on earth."

Jamie said Brandon said to her, "You're going to write all this down, right?"

Jamie turned her head slightly and said, "Yes, Brandon, if you would just relax for a minute we're getting there, we're getting there."

"I'm running out of time," Jamie said Brandon said to her urgently.

"You are not running out of time," Jamie to him. Then she looked at me and smiled and said, "He's laughing at me." She said he was saying, "Come on, it's me, I'm running out of time.

We only have an hour to talk." Jamie said he wanted to talk as much as possible while I was there because he had a lot to tell me.

"Are you going to allow any other family members to speak?" Jamie asked him.

"They're all here," he explained, "but don't worry, they don't need to say anything."

"Really, so you think you're the "center of the show?" Jamie replied.

"I am!" Brandon said.

"He's talking so fast I get lost," Jamie said.

"Where would you like to start?" I asked Jamie to ask Brandon.

"Well, we need to start with saying I love you," Brandon said to me through Jamie.

"I love you too," I replied.

"Who's the best mom in the world?" Brandon said.

"Are you still okay?" I asked. I wasn't asking because I thought he wasn't okay; somehow I had to reestablish, for my own clarity, that he was all right so I could be all right. I think it was difficult for me to grasp that he was really gone but he was also still here and this was the way we were going to communicate.

"Yes!" Brandon answered. "I'm fine. I'm feeling great. Everything is fine. Actually I feel better as the days go on, because I have more of a grasp on how to talk with you. I know you're hearing me. There are times when I say something [when I'm around you and Jamie's not there to translate] like "Cool!" and you just kind of stop in your tracks. I don't know if you're hearing my words verbatim. I really think you're feeling them more than hearing them even though you don't know that's what's going on. I'm trying and working really hard, Mom. I'm giving you the words in your chest."

I didn't know what he meant by that but I imagined him somehow putting his message inside me in a way I couldn't understand.

"Because that's the way I get the biggest reaction out of you," Brandon went on through Jamie. "I just push it into you. It makes you stop what you're doing and makes you think about me."

"I'm learning," he went on. Jamie reported Brandon had kind of a smug, happy-with-himself look. "I do feel better that we have that. But you really need to get off my case."

"Why?" I asked.

"You're asking me to do more. Show you more or give you more signs."

Jamie asked me if that was true.

"Are you talking about the dimes?" I asked Brandon. I explained to Jamie that we had found over 150 dimes in the last eighteen months.

"Holy cow!" Jamie exclaimed.

"Why the dimes?" I asked Brandon.

"Like I said, I want you to be rich! I want to take care of you, but also the number ten is round."

Jamie told me Brandon was showing her a bunch of pictures. That's sometimes the way he communicates to Jamie, by showing her visions.

"It looks like a parking lot, a hallway, underneath a chair. Maybe I'm in a restaurant or something. It looks like a wooden slatted chair. Dirt or sand?" She addressed Brandon: "Why the images? Is it where you leave the dimes?" She turned back to me. "So you're really finding them not in places where you would lose a dime out of your pocket? You are actually finding them in really odd places?"

"Yes. I found one that washed up on the shore in the ocean."

"You found a dime in the ocean? How do you find a dime in the ocean?"

"It washed up on the shore."

"Now he's rubbing his hands together," Jamie reported.

"It's magic," Brandon said.

"It's not magic," Jamie said.

"I've figured out how to do it," Brandon said.

I remembered something Jamie had said a few minutes ago and posed a question to her: "When he was showing you all the images of dirt and sand and slatted chairs, was he referring to the golf tournament we had in his honor?"

Two months ago, at the end of May, we organized a golf tournament at the Montezuma country club golf course. We named it the Brando Open and used it, along with an auction and evening meal, to raise money in Brandon's honor, with all proceeds going back to the community. Donations came pouring in; teams filled up quickly and the turnout was amazing. We raised over $25,000. The money was used for resurfacing the Montezuma High School baseball field, buying a weight board for the weight room at the high school, and giving college scholarships to high school seniors—Kenny invested part of the money for an on-going scholarship program. We also donated some of the money for a crucifix at our church.

"I thought it was awesome," Brandon said now through Jamie. "It was *killer.*"

"Did he actually say killer?" I asked Jamie. That was the exact word he used to use to describe something he approved of immensely.

"Killer was the exact word, killer," Jamie said.

I couldn't believe I could actually hear him talking the way he always talked. It felt like warm water defrosting my frozen heart—I knew he was there with me.

I told Jamie about how Father Nick, who led the opening prayer at the golf tournament, found a dime in the gravel in the parking lot when he was leaving. He knew about Brandon's dimes and came back, found me among the crowd, and gave me the dime.

"I think [Father Nick] is such a cool guy," Jamie reported Brandon said. "He's helped our family so much. Not only in the religious way, also in a spiritual way. He is a very unique guy. Thank God we have him on our side."

"Does Brandon come to see us often at home?" I asked Jamie to ask him.

"All the time. I have to, or else you'll kick my butt. Otherwise you'll chew me out. You have to stop being so hard on me."

"That's not being hard," Jamie said to Brandon. "That's her checking in on you, wanting to know where you are and what you're doing. That's being a mom!" Looking back on this meeting now I see that Jamie and Brandon were also establishing their relationship.

"As long as I know he's in heaven I'm fine," I said.

Jamie told me that Brandon was pretending he was raising the roof with his hands into the air saying, "I'm in heaven."

"The funny thing is, Mom," he went on. "Heaven's not up there. So you can stop looking up!" I started laughing and told Jamie that I do that all the time. "Just look straight ahead. We share the same space," Brandon said.

"It's nice to hear him say that," Jamie said. "We do share the same space. That's why we run into each other so much!"

"I believe that we do share the same space, only we're on different planes," I said.

"Different dimensions," Brandon corrected. There he was—my son. Correcting me in a good-natured way, just like he always did.

"Is Henrietta (my paternal grandmother) still there?" I asked Jamie to ask Brandon.

"Yes. I can't shake her," he replied. Then Jamie said Brandon turned to his great-grandmother and said, "Well, are you going to tell her you're here?"

"You said nobody but you was going to talk," she replied to Brandon. I could see that the two of them were teasing each other, bickering in a joking sort of way. That was another thing Brandon loved to do.

"She can really put her thumb on it," he said. "Why are you looking at me, Jamie?"

"Because you're the one doing all the talking," Jamie said.

"Go ahead, Grandma, talk! She can really be a thorn! I can understand why someone would love her so much, but I can understand why someone would want to run away from her too," Brandon said affectionately.

"Your grandmother is saying she really loves you," Jamie passed on to me. "She said she really loved the flowers you put on her grave on Memorial Day."

After my first meeting with Jamie, when I found out that my grandmother Henrietta was the one who met Brandon when he passed to the other side, I made a beautiful heart out of red roses and put it on her grave to show her how grateful I was and how much I loved her for what she'd done for Brandon.

"She is really dressed for this occasion," Jamie went on to say, "like she is dressed to be here and to be seen. She has on a nice polka-dot blouse and gold jewelry."

"Is my dad still here?" I asked Jamie.

"Yes, your dad is standing in the back and he's waving now. He's got a great smile. His whole face lights up when he smiles. He looks like a 1950s classic movie star. All of the other spirits are still here also. Brandon is still sitting by you on the edge of the couch."

I asked her to describe to me what Brandon looked like that day. Jamie told me he looked fit and was wearing blue jeans and tennis shoes. "Are you an athlete?" she asked Brandon.

She listened to his answer and then said, "That's funny. He's saying, 'I'm not an athlete in the sense that you're thinking of, but I do play sports.'"

Brandon had loved sports from the time he was old enough to pick up a bat and ball. The first thing he did in the morning when he was two years old was grab his cowboy boots and put them on—the boots came halfway up his chubby little legs—then he grabbed a plastic toy bat and plastic ball and headed outside to play. His dad played fast-pitch softball in the summer and when Brandon was four he always brought his glove to the games and walked around to every team member and asked if they would play catch with him; he never gave up until he found someone who said yes. When he got older he spent hours in the driveway picking up rocks and batting them across the road into the cornfield. He had excellent hand-eye coordination, even at a very young age. He made our front yard into a baseball field: Home plate was a large dirt area by the big oak tree, the smaller tree was second base and the front step was third. He was the pitcher, the hitter and the commentator. He grew to love all competitive sports and became a walking sports statistic encyclopedia.

Another question came to my mind to ask Brandon. "Can you tell that I've been sad lately?" I asked him.

"Yes," Brandon said. "Mom, you're sad because a year has gone by, and I think you're just realizing another year is going to go by the same way. I think you just finally understood that I'm not coming back through the door. It's okay though, because I'm coming back in the door a different way."

"He's fighting back emotions." Jamie told me. I was too; I started to cry.

"I told you I'd never leave you alone," Brandon said through Jamie.

Brandon started addressing the worries I'd been talking about with Kathy in the car on the way to Atlanta—my sadness because his life had been cut short and he was missing out on having a wife and family—without my saying anything about it now, as if he could read my mind or was there in the car with us earlier. "I don't feel I've missed out on anything in life," he said. "Not having a wife or children. None of that, I missed none of it. Because the love that I had with my family and with my mom was real and was honest." Jamie reported that Brandon put his finger up in the air. "Very honest."

Jamie giggled. "Apparently he could tell you anything. Maybe too much of some things."

"That's true," I said, thinking about how Brandon used to tell me about his escapades with his friends and his drama with girlfriends—how this one wanted to date him and how he didn't want to get serious; he always had long funny stories. "Some things I didn't want to know, Brandon," I said, laughing and crying.

"That talking fulfilled me, and I didn't have the need to find it anywhere else. What I do have a need for is to find a way to communicate with you again."

Brandon and Jamie and I talked a bit about the book I was writing, even though at that point I barely had a book— I was just journaling. But Brandon seemed to know that the book was real and would be published. Jamie said that there were many spirits who were excited that I was writing about Brandon and his experience in the afterlife because in a way his story was also their story. "I have never met a group of people, of spirits, who have such a plan for somebody like they have for you," Jamie said. "The book is just the first part. Would you mind if your new job in life was to be a messenger [for people in the afterlife]?" Jamie asked me.

I said that I would be happy to have that be the case.

Brandon said I should write in my book about what I went through with grief. "Don't think there will be a day when you can talk about it and not cry," Brandon went on through Jamie. "But the crying is different each time. Sometimes you cry because it's sad, it's because you never wanted it to happen. Sometimes you cry because you're not in control. Sometimes you cry because you do really miss me."

"Were you sad when you were here on earth?" I asked Brandon.

"The normal sadness stuff, but no severe depression." Jamie reported that he gave her a smug look and said to her, "Depression? Over what? I had nothing to be depressed about." All he had, he said to me through Jamie, was ordinary sadness, when he didn't get a certain toy, or he wasn't allowed to golf, or the weather was bad, or the girl didn't like him, or the date went really wrong. "I had a few of those!" he said to Jamie laughing. "That was my sadness, Mom. I was never depressed. I would have told you. As I said, I told you everything." Jamie said that Brandon whispered in a very sweet, very soft voice, under his breath, "I love you."

Then something occurred to me. "Ask him about when I'm out on my deck and I think about him. The wind starts blowing through the trees," I said to Jamie.

"I don't see the trees, but I see the wind! The wind, the wind, the wind!" Jamie said, describing what Brandon was showing her. "Did he ever do drama class? He's a ham!" Jamie said smiling.

"Yes, he had a passion for acting," I said.

"I should have done it for a living," Brandon said.

In June of the year he died Brandon had a lead part in a community play, "Lie, Cheat, and Genuflect," performed in a dinner theater in a town about fourteen miles away from us. Because he wanted to go into acting, he entered a talent search in Des Moines that year and was chosen to go to New York and model during the summer. He hated the modeling and didn't want his dad or any of his friends to know about it, because he had to model a pair of skimpy swim trunks on the runway. But he did it because he thought it could be a way to break into acting because talent scouts attended the shows. In October I took him to Chicago and the modeling agency we'd signed up with took photos of him beside Lake Michigan, on the campus of Loyola, and in other settings around Chicago, and used the pictures to create a portfolio.

"You did runway stuff?" Jamie asked Brandon now.

She said Brandon told her how embarrassed he was to walk down the runway in a pair of skimpys. She teased him about wearing a Speedo and he told her that she could use it as a slingshot.

I told him that when Cody and I were sorting through his stuff a couple of weeks ago, we laughed and cried at the same time. About half the things we found didn't even belong to him. Cody kept saying, 'I wondered where that shirt went.' I said that we kept most of his clothes and we often wear them, but nobody wears the Speedo.

Jamie said that Brandon's interest in theater made sense. "He's very animated!"

"I loved every minute of it!" she said Brandon said. And then he added, somewhat cryptically, "Now the whole world is my stage."

The rest of the hour-and-forty-five-minute session passed quickly.

"Everyone's saying goodbye, except for Brandon. Brandon's blowing kisses," Jamie said.

Blowing kisses came to be Brandon's way of saying goodbye at the end of all my sessions with Jamie. He told Jamie to tell me he didn't want to say good-bye. And once in a later session he said to me, "My kisses are mortar to fill the cracks in your heart."

CHAPTER 6

THE PENDULUM

During that meeting in Atlanta, Jamie told me about a way I could communicate with Brandon myself when I got back home. She said I could do it using a simple pendulum.

"They're not high tech," she said. "This is what I teach my classes with." She handed me a piece of fishing line with a washer tied on the end. "This particular string is really long but the string really only has to be about six to eight inches long. A pendulum can be made with anything, even just a ring and a string. You hold it so the ring is about an inch over your open hand." Jamie told me that to communicate with Brandon this way I should ask yes or no questions and wait for the pendulum to spin around above my hand. I'd have to figure out through trial and error what spin meant yes, what meant no, and what meant ask again. "If it's spinning very slowly, then you can say to the person make it bigger. Then when you say thank you, the thing will actually stop."

I took the pendulum from Jamie, held it so the washer was an inch over the palm of my hand, and asked Brandon what my yes-spin was going to be. The washer on the end of the fishing line shook, as if it was vibrating with energy— I was holding my hand perfectly still—then the washer turned slowly in a counter-clockwise circle. I knew that meant my yes-spin was going to be counter-clockwise.

'Then ask, what is your no?" Jamie instructed me.

When I asked Brandon what my no was the washer started shaking even more than it had when I asked about my yes.

"It's shaking like crazy! I'm holding my hand perfectly still," I said.

"It's taking a lot of energy-pulling to make that thing shake!" Jamie said. "Brandon, you have to give a different no, don't use the shake, you have to make it broader and bigger."

The washer started moving diagonally back and forth across the palm of my hand.

"My no is across the width of my hand," I said.

"That's a good no," Jamie said. "Wild, isn't it?"

She told me we needed to figure out something Brandon could do with the pendulum that meant either ask the question again or the question isn't clear. "The hardest thing about using the pendulum is asking a good question," she said. For example, she explained, if you ask two questions the person on the other side can't answer with a simple yes or no. "What is your symbol for repeat the question?" Jamie said.

The pendulum started shaking again. I was still holding my hand out. "Look at that!" I said. "Is that my ask-the-question-again sign?

"Don't use the shaking, Brandon. Use a different sign," Jamie instructed Brandon. "That's a lot of energy shaking, that! It's funny what he's saying," Jamie said. "He's saying, 'I'm not making it shake. I'm trying to make it stand still. That's an option, Jamie. Absence of movement, that's a choice."

Brandon was arguing with Jamie, as if he knew more than she did. Which, once again, was totally like him. That was Brandon's personality shining through. Loud, clear, and adamant.

"All right, you! Absence of movement, that's your choice," Jamie said, relenting.

"Okay, okay, you win, Brandon!" I shouted and started laughing.

Jamie went on to explain that I would have to ask those questions for several weeks, each time I picked up my pendulum—what is my yes, et cetera—but then I wouldn't have to do that any more. I could just say, "I lost my keys. Are they in this room?" or "Brandon, are you here?"

Jamie told me Brandon said that we should use the pendulum when I felt his presence but didn't know what he was trying to tell me. "The thing you lack, Mom," Brandon said through Jamie, "is confirmation. There is nobody standing around you saying, Yup, you're right. So now you can pick up the pendulum and I can answer, 'Yes, I am giving you a message.'"

When I got home the first thing I did was try the pendulum out. I went into the living room alone and took out the pendulum Jamie gave me, made of two washers tied to the end of a piece of fishing line. I took off my shoes and socks and sat cross-legged in the recliner. Then I picked up the pendulum and dangled the washers about an inch above my open palm. I anchored my arm by putting my right elbow on the arm of the chair. I asked Brandon if he was there with me. The washers started shaking, they began slowly moving in a small counter-clockwise circle. I felt thrilled. There was a tingling sensation on the left side of my palm near my thumb and I knew it came from

Brandon—Jamie had told me I'd feel a sensation that was different from normal, and now here it was.

I told Brandon I loved him and the washer moved faster in larger circles. I felt even more thrilled. I asked him a few more questions—whether he was okay, whether we would keep doing this, and he answered yes to everything.

I've been using the pendulum to communicate with Brandon ever since, for six years now. At first I did it weekly, now I probably do it every couple of weeks, often when something comes up I need an answer to. I sit barefoot and cross-legged in the recliner every time, and every time the circle gets faster and bigger when I tell Brandon I love him. There are times when I ask him whether people's intentions are good or whether I should do something I secretly know I shouldn't, and the answer always comes promptly: a firm no in the form of the washer crossing the width my palm.

The pendulum is a great tool, but eventually, after using it a lot for a couple of years, I found I didn't need to rely on it as much. Now I feel like I can kind of hear Brandon sometimes in a subtle way, like a quiet little voice that pops into my head. Often it says, "Really, Mom? You don't have to ask me that. You already know the answer to that."

Whenever that happens I say, out loud, "I know," and then I picture Brandon's grinning face.

Chapter 7

Still in the Picture

In addition to sending us dimes and dreams and communicating with us through Jamie, and communicating with me through the pendulum and maybe telepathy, Brandon has found a way to make his presence known sometimes in the pictures we take. We first noticed it in some digital photos taken at Cody and Britni's wedding in November of 2010.

My friend Kathy took most of the pictures at the wedding, and at the reception she told me that when she was taping the wedding ceremony, small orbs of white light kept showing up, coming and going, in the video camera viewfinder, and when she played the video back afterwards she saw them again. It happened again when she was taking pictures with two different digital cameras. We all looked at the photos on one of the cameras and there they were: white, hazy, perfectly round circles in four of the pictures taken of Kenny's extended family standing together outside the place where the reception was held. When we printed the pictures when we got back to Iowa after the wedding we saw the circles even more clearly. In three of the photos the circle was hovering above Kenny's dad, Grandpa Smith's, head. In the fourth picture the circle was on the opposite end of the group, next to Kenny's oldest brother, Mike. Everyone in the family agreed that the orbs must've been signs from Brandon, or even photos of Brandon's energy that he was somehow projecting into the pictures.

Somehow I never thought to mention the orbs the next time I talked to Brandon and Jamie, after we noticed them following the wedding. Maybe because we were focusing on the dolphins— a pod of dolphins showed up in the water the night before Cody's wedding on St. John's and we were sure they had something to do with Brandon too. In our family's excitement about the dolphins, we kind of forgot about the orbs in the pictures.

Then some more orbs showed up in some photos taken of me when I went to Florida with friends in March 2013. My friend's daughter, Ashley, took three pictures of me with her phone and in every picture a large white hazy circular orb surrounded part of my image. Ashley noticed it and said, "Look at these pictures." It was a beautiful evening, no rain or wind. You couldn't ignore the orbs in the photos because they were so obvious. In one picture the orb looked like a giant halo surrounding my entire upper body. Somebody else sat in my seat and Ashley took a picture of her and the orb didn't show up in that picture.

"Brandon never wants to miss out on a vacation to the beach," I said, laughing, when Ashley showed me the first picture. (We used to take Brandon and our other kids to that same beach when they were little.)

My friend Debbie got kind of freaked out by the orbs in the photos. I've come to take signs from Brandon for granted— or at least not think they're a very big deal—but when I stop to think about it I realize they are a big deal and not everybody will feel the same way about them that I do.

Debbie jumped up and said, "Let's go to dinner." She looked pale during dinner and has never mentioned the orbs in the pictures again.

Since that time we continue to see orbs in many of the family pictures we take. Brandon wants to make sure we know he's traveling with us. When I asked him about the orbs, during a meeting with Jamie in December of 2013, he started laughing, paused, and said, "It's me!"

Whether it's through orbs that show up in our pictures or messages passed on by Jamie or a quiet little voice that pops into my head or a dime that shows up in the middle of the living room floor in a pivotal or difficult moment, I know it's coming from Brandon.

I've been having phone meetings with Jamie four times a year since that meeting with her in Atlanta. I'm often amazed by the timing of the dates when I meet with her. The dates are picked for me randomly by her assistant, but they almost always turn out to be something significant, as if they're being orchestrated from the beyond.　For example, one date fell on my granddaughter McKinli's first birthday; another was the day Calvin was born; another was on the day before we left for Jessica's wedding. Sometimes the appointments come when I'm especially needing confirmation that Brandon is still alive, still with us, like the time the date fell on the day before the sixth anniversary of his passing.

Every single time I meet with Jamie she says something, usually many things, that could only come from Brandon.

I'm continually struck and delighted by the things he says through her. Once we were talking about something I was concerned about regarding a family friend. I said that I try to see the good in everyone, and Brandon said, "There goes my mother, Miss Positive." Jamie said he threw his arm out as if I was passing by him and he was pointing to me. I was amused that Brandon still knows me so well. I was also comforted by the fact that he's still real, still down to earth, still— once again—himself.

Chapter 8

Spare a Square

When I returned from Atlanta I was very excited to share my conversation with Brandon with my family, and Kenny, Cody, Jessica, and Britni were all anxious to hear about it. When I told them what Brandon had to say through Jamie, Cody said he wanted to make an appointment with Jamie himself and have his own conversation with his brother. But it was more than a year before that happened. Not long after I went to Atlanta and met with Jamie, Cody and Britni got engaged, then they got married about twelve months later. Their wedding was in St. Thomas and we were all busy getting ready for it. Cody finally got an appointment with Jamie in December of 2010, about a month after his wedding.

Cody called Jamie from his house and talked to her—and Brandon—alone. Jamie took notes of everything Brandon said during the meeting with Cody, typed them up, and emailed them to Cody, who forwarded them to me. I have the notes on the desk in front of me now—reading them is almost like hearing Brandon's voice talking.

The very first word that Brandon said to Cody through Jamie was "dork," a name Brandon always called his younger brother. I remember Brandon tapping Cody on the forehead and saying, "dork stamp," when they were passing each other in the hallway at home. Jamie had no way of knowing that, and Cody told me after his meeting with her that when the first word she passed on to him from Brandon was dork, he knew, without a shadow of a doubt, that it was his brother talking to him from the other side.

At the beginning of the call Cody had told Jamie he was nervous and was feeling guilty about not reaching out to Brandon sooner. Brandon said now through Jamie, "I'm nervous too, don't worry." Then he added jokingly, in typical Brandon language, preserved by Jamie in her notes, "But ya know I know so much about you, I guess if I were you I would be scared too. Dude, you are doing stuff I never thought you would do, yeah, Mr. Straight Lace." (Brandon was referring to the fact that Cody has always been a bit straight-laced, especially compared to him. I don't know exactly what Brandon meant by "stuff" that Cody was doing, but I'm sure Cody knows.)

One of the first questions Cody asked Brandon was, "Were you there at the wedding?"

The reply was, "Not only was I at your wedding, I stayed for the whole thing and I left you a sign before you got married, that is how amazing I am."

"You mean the dolphins turning up?" Cody asked.

We had rented two sailboats for a sunset cruise to the island of St. John for the wedding rehearsal dinner. As we were traveling along in the boats, a pod of dolphins appeared on both sides of each boat. They were swirling, turning on their sides and their backs, as if to say look at us showing off. It was almost as if they were leading us. The crew was amazed. They told us dolphins were rarely around in this area because the water was too warm for them and that they hadn't seen any dolphins for eight years. We were also told that seeing dolphins was a sign of good luck.

As soon as the dolphins showed up—it was as if they appeared out of nowhere, on both sides of both boats—Britni and I looked at each other and got teary eyed. We'd known Brandon wouldn't let this event happen without letting us know he was with us. He likes to make his impression in a big way.

"Yeah, dude," Brandon confirmed through Jamie for Cody. "That was a sign of love. I got them to come in because you have to know that you are blessed, it was *amazing*. There were people crying, man, it was *awesome*." Once again, this was exactly Brandon's voice coming through in Jamie's notes. I knew it was him talking when I read those notes and I still do, and that makes me smile.

Brandon had lots to say about Cody's choice of wife. "All I have to say is you picked the right girl, or should I say, she picked you. You will be married forever, no divorce in this love story. She is going to rock your world because she is going to start to organize now and nest and then ask for the babies. She is on a time schedule. Everything she wants is in good taste, so you will want it too."

Everything Brandon predicted during that session with Cody came true: Britni is very organized, and she and Cody have had babies—two of them—and now they've each started their own businesses.

Cody told Brandon how much he missed him and Brandon

said, "Man, I miss you! God, we could laugh so freakin' hard we would bust." (It's still amazing to me to read these words on a piece of paper, typed out by Jamie—words that come from Brandon, whom I thought I had lost and would never, ever hear speak again.)

Then Brandon said another thing that sounded just like him, and that also gives a clue about his life in the afterlife: "But now I got these super human powers to know the future and shit like that." It's interesting to me that while he does seem to have "super powers" of a sort, as he says, he's still totally himself. Jamie included two smiling emoticons in the transcript to indicate that Brandon was laughing in this moment. Cody told me later that he didn't think Brandon had any more super powers than any other spirit on the other side, Brandon just loved to laugh about his super powers, like he had one up on you. That was just like Brandon too—he was always joking about his own powers, it was his way of affectionately teasing people.

At the time Cody met with Jamie, he was carrying around a lot of guilty feelings about the night Brandon passed. Brandon and Joshua, the friend Brandon was with when he died, had called Cody's cell phone earlier that night and left him a message asking him to come out and have a beer with them at a bar. Joshua made the call but Cody could hear Brandon belly-laughing in the background at everything Joshua was saying. Cody said he didn't take the call because he had to be to work at five o'clock the next morning and didn't want to go out that night. When Cody talked to Brandon during his session with Jamie, he voiced his guilty feelings about not being there that night. Brandon's reply was this: "The night that I died, I am so happy that you did not come out and play. Boy oh boy destiny had her claws in me. But I am cool with it now, I know that it was my place and my time."

"You should have called me to pick you up, I should have been there," Cody said.

"I didn't think I should have called you to pick me up. I had a ride," Brandon said through Jamie. Cody told me later, after Jamie had sent me her typed notes from the meeting, that he felt so much better after the meeting—he had always felt like Brandon might still be alive if he had been there that night to babysit for him. (This is the word Brandon would want him to use to describe what he felt like he should have done that night, and it's the word Cody would have used for it too.) Cody also said he'd had a lingering fear that Brandon was mad at him, and these feelings were the main reason he wanted to meet with Jamie. The meeting totally reassured him and wildly exceeded his expectations.

Later on in the meeting, Cody brought up something else that was weighing heavily on him. The last time Cody saw Brandon they came to our house for a spaghetti dinner. They often bantered back and forth at the dinner table, typical sibling arguing. That night Cody came in a 2004 Ford 150 pickup he was thinking about buying and wanted his dad's input about. He drove it over and we all went for a ride in it, Cody, Kenny, Brandon, and myself. We came home after the test drive and the boys started eating. Brandon was chomping loudly and it was annoying Cody. So of course Cody said to Brandon, "Quit chomping so loud." The argument escalated between them with some name-calling and some not-so-nice words exchanged.

When Cody brought that night up while having his conversation with Brandon, this is what Brandon had to say to him through Jamie: "Spaghetti at Mom and Dad's? Yeah. I remember you rode the truck over and you didn't tell me that you were going to bring it." Brandon made a wry comment about his own, old car: "I was still driving my green Ford Taurus. Now who's embarrassed? I am." Brandon went on. "You wanted to let me have it that night and kept pushing at me. You didn't let up about the way I was chomping my food. I knew you and I were okay. This was not a special night. This was something we did a lot. It never weighed heavy on my heart. I know it weighs heavily for you, but just because I left the next day. At least you heard me laughing last." Here Brandon was referring to the voicemail message he and Joshua left Cody the night Brandon died, in which Cody could hear Brandon laughing in the background. (This block of conversation is one among many that convinces me that the messages Jamie passes on to us from Brandon are the real thing. There's no way that Jamie could have known the details about the spaghetti dinner, the "chomping" criticism, the kind of car Brandon had, the way that Cody kept pushing Brandon that night, and the way he'd been feeling ever since.)

After Cody and Brandon talked about what happened the night Brandon died, Cody said, "I have a question for you."

"Hit me," Brandon said.

"Knowing all the people that loved you and want to see you on this side, and after being on the other side in the afterlife, would you come back here to be with me and Mom and Dad and Jess if you could?" Cody asked.

Brandon repeated the question back to Cody. "Knowing what I know now would I come back? I hope you won't be disappointed, buddy, but I would not. This place is amazing. It fills every crevice in my being. I never felt like that, and I know it's why I drank. I was trying to fill a void, but I didn't know how deep it was.

"Fun is my drug now though," Brandon went on. (In a future meeting, Jamie said to me, about Brandon's humor, "It clearly comes from a fun place, it's not manipulative, and is done to be funny with a positive viewpoint. Even when we're talking about struggling and grieving, his outlook is that everything is good.")

Cody went on to ask Brandon his next question. "Will I see you when I die?"

Once again Brandon repeated Cody's question back to him. "Will you see me when you die?

"Dude, when you open your eyes from death, you will see my entire face right up in yours. So I will be the one to carry you over, and what is great is, you will be old and I will still be looking good. You worry about what you're going to look like— you will be just like Dad and Grandpa Smith, with a gut and no hair.

"You better start working out," Brandon added. "I'm serious, man. Your body is your temple, treat it right. Run, why don't you run? Get some good music and run—that always kept you in shape. You need balance though with eating and working out. Stop being neurotic, you've become more neurotic. Go work out with Brit, dude, you know that's what she wants you to do." Then

Brandon paused to rib Cody, in his typical jesting Brandon way. "Brit is definitely better looking than you. You upgraded when you married her." It's this and other things like it that let me know this is Brandon talking—this is *exactly* what he would say.

It was also just like Brandon to tell his younger brother what he needed to do. But it was good advice and such important things Cody needed to hear. He did hear, too: Since his meeting with Brandon he's been working out and doing many other things to take care of his body.

"For your health," Brandon went on, "you need to take some vitamins, D especially to help with your digestion, because you are getting older. You're eating too much meat and your body can't digest well enough, so eat smaller portions. You'll feel better, trust me." This is something that Brandon wouldn't have said when he was among us—he was a meat and potato eater too, like their father and grandfather, all of them good farm boys. The fact that Brandon told Cody to cut down on meat reminds me that he does have new information and insights in the place he's in now. On the other hand, telling someone to cut down on meat and eat smaller portions isn't exactly radical advice; I eat that way myself because I know it's better for me.

"So it means you have to take care of yourself," Brandon concluded his health advice.

Cody asked Jamie to ask Brandon, "Do you have anything to say to Mom, Dad or Jessica?"

"Well, tell them I'm still here in all my glory, and still checking in on everyone," Brandon said with his typical confident fun-loving pride.

"How often are you with me?" Cody asked.

"At least once a day, but I give you signs like once a week, so you know that I'm around."

"Do you remember that Christmas Eve when we stayed awake all night?" Cody asked Brandon.

"You mean when we stayed up all night and watched Seinfeld?" Brandon said through Jamie, offering another detail there's no way Jamie could have known.

"Yeah, we ate, drank and trashed Mom's living room," Brandon went on.

"I know, I know, you watch [Seinfeld] every night [now.] Sometimes I sit with you. You know all the stupid sayings too. I love it! I love it!" And here Brandon said—here I see, typed on the page by Jamie—something that really floors me: "Spare a square."

Jamie asked Cody, "Do you know what that means? I don't know what that means."

Cody started laughing and said, "I know exactly what that means." He told me later, when we were talking about this meeting, that he went on to explain to Jamie that "spare a square" comes from one of his and Brandon's favorite Seinfeld episodes. In that episode Elaine, one of the main characters, realizes there's no toilet paper in a public bathroom stall and calls out to the woman in the stall beside her, "Spare a square?" The woman refuses, of course. The boys always found this hilarious.

"Oh," Jamie said. "I get it. Now Brandon's showing me an image of Elaine with toilet paper wrapped up all over her, that she stole."

Then Jamie told Cody that Brandon was laughing and

that he said, "I love those shows. We could do this all day."

Cody told me today that staying up all night watching Seinfeld with Brandon that time was the best Christmas moment he and his brother ever shared. He also said that since Brandon passed he's been watching Brandon's old Seinfeld DVDs every night, the way Brandon himself used to watch Seinfeld every night, and that doing that makes him feel close to his brother because he feels like Brandon is sitting there with him, watching too.

"Is heaven amazing?" Cody asked Brandon.

Brandon's reply was, "Yes, heaven is *amazing*."

"Will I be there?" Cody asked.

"Yes, you will come here, there's no other place to go," Brandon replied. "There is no hell, and nothing to fear except the idea of fear itself." He went on to describe what he's experienced in the afterlife: "There's no pain. Nothing. Pure energy. Pure memory. I have all I need. Even if I want to be upset, I can't seem to muster it up. That's how beautiful this place is." He commented further on hell. "If you wanna talk about hell, well, you're already in it. Life on earth is the farthest you can be from where I am. Life on earth is hell. You found happiness there on earth, so just imagine what you can find here."

Cody's time with Jamie was almost over. "I can't wait for you to be a dad," Brandon said, winding up the conversation. "Kiss Brit for me and tell her I've got her back. I love you so much. Thank you for reaching out finally."

"I probably waited too long to reach out to you," Cody said.

"No. It wasn't too long of a wait, but I'm really excited that you did."

I was floored by the very last thing my two sons talked about during Cody's session with Jamie, and I still find it amusing and slightly astonishing.

"One more thing, Brandon," Cody said. "I'm sorry I don't go to the cemetery very often to visit your grave, it's not something I feel comfortable doing."

"Don't be sorry," Brandon said through Jamie. "My grave spooks me out too. She put my image all over it." She, he was referring me of course. I had a picture of Brandon printed on a bronze plate and then had it screwed onto his headstone.

"I know," Cody said.

"No, man, it's creepy, sorry. Please don't tell her that. Please. She's going to be pissed if she knows that. Yeah, it was creepy. Geez."

When Cody and I were talking and laughing about this recently, Cody said it was just like Brandon to say that about his picture on his gravestone and then to say in the next breath, as he did, "But damn, I look good."

Cody's meeting with Brandon and Jamie made him really happy and after that his heart was at ease. He continues to talk to his brother every three months. (So do I, in separate sessions.) He says those meetings make him feel close to his brother and like his brother isn't gone. My meetings with Brandon make me feel the same way. Most of all, I'm amazed at the way Brandon is still Brandon—his personality, his language and ways of talking, everything about him, shines through in those phone meetings with Jamie.

CHAPTER 9

"I'M ALIVE! I'M ALIVE!"

"I'm alive! I'm alive!" Brandon said when I had my phone meeting with Jamie this past April.

Jamie had started the meeting by telling me that on her way into her office that morning her car's gas gauge had started out with only thirteen miles worth of gas, then it plummeted to five miles worth of gas after she drove only a hundred feet, then it shot up to fourteen miles worth of gas after she drove two hundred yards. She heard laughter, not literally but psychically, the way she hears things. She looked at her iPhone to see who she was seeing that day and saw my name as the first client of the day. "Then Brandon let me know it was him playing a trick on me," she said.

I laughed and said that it was just like Brandon to pull a prank like that. When he was alive he prided himself on being the ultimate prankster. He would do anything to get me in a flustered state. Once, after I put a casserole I was taking to a potluck on the backseat and told Brandon and Cody to be careful to not let it spill, Brandon gave Cody a signal, whispered, "Watch this, Mom will start to yell," then said in a startled voice, "Mom, this stuff just spilled all over back here!" When I started screaming they both started laughing and said, "Just kidding." Brandon was very proud of the joke he'd just pulled.

I could see now that he was still a comedian, always laughing at some affectionate joke on you and then taking a little bow.

Jamie added that when she got to her office she found a dime in the middle of her office floor and then remembered that Brandon was "the dime guy." She said the year on the dime was 1996, and I remembered that 1996 was the year Jessica graduated from high school; now Jessica was getting married on May 1st.

I started off the reading by asking Brandon how he was and that's when Jamie reported he said, "I'm alive! I'm alive!" She added that he sounded like Christopher Walken when he said it, like it was some sort of grandiose declaration.

Once again that mischievous personality of Brandon's was coming though. Hearing him talk through Jamie always makes me smile. I know it's definitely Brandon talking, and therefore I believe, beyond a shadow of doubt, that he truly is still alive. He's still there, somehow, in some realm or spiritual dimension many people don't even believe exists. ("Dimension" is the word Brandon uses for it.)

Brandon refers to his transition to the other side as *coming home*. I find it very interesting that that's what he calls death. It seems exactly the opposite of how most people in this world think about death, but it makes more sense if Brandon and everyone else who has passed really is still alive. Brandon told me that dying is like being born. It doesn't hurt and we should all stop worrying about it.

Over the years since I've been communicating with him on the other side, I've come to feel—really, truly, through-and-through—that he is very close by, close to me, even though I can't physically see him. Once when we were talking in a meeting with Jamie about how ornery he still is, he said, through her, "If I was angel boy you'd say, 'Where's my son?' You wouldn't even recognize me." I felt like I could almost see the twinkly little gleam in his eyes at that moment.

Brandon seems pleased, too, that we're still talking, still carrying on a real relationship, that he's still part of the family. "This is how life should be for every dead and living relationship," he said once during a session with Jamie. "We should just be in conversation all the time, instead of 'close the door and make it go away.'" Once he said, "Say my name," meaning that we shouldn't be afraid to talk about him during everyday life. My family isn't afraid to talk about Brandon—we do it a lot and we always will, my little grandchildren even talk about him, saying his name and pointing at his picture. But many people who have experienced the death of a loved one do stop talking about that person, as if that person is truly gone and even saying their name is painful. Brandon says that isn't good for anyone. He's still alive and so is everyone else who's passed.

Sometimes Brandon does seem to feel a little regret about leaving us—for our sakes, not his. When Kenny and I met with Jamie about a year and a half ago the conversation turned to the accident that killed Brandon. Brandon was saying through Jamie, "I was horsing around and it was so stupid. How many times did you tell me, Mom, throughout my whole life, not to touch this or not to touch that, but that was my personality." He got really quiet for a while and it seemed to me that he was feeling regret about what he'd done—once again, not on his own behalf but because of the repercussions on this side.

I jumped in, trying to make him feel better. "Don't worry, we'll all be together someday soon."

Brandon's mood suddenly changed. Now he seemed resistant to the idea of us joining him soon. He acted like he wanted to make sure we knew we were going to have long lives. And maybe like he needed more time in the afterlife without us being there with him. *"Whoa, whoa, whoa. Not too soon. Take your time, I need a bit of a break."*

"Yeah, Brandon," Kenny said laughing. "If you think Great-grandma's controlling [there in the afterlife], wait till your mom gets there. You'll never be left alone."

Even with Brandon in the afterlife Brandon and Kenny were still ganging up on me in their teasing way and all I could do was laugh. "Very funny, you two," I said. "My health must be good then if I'm not coming to see you soon."

"Yes, Mom, your health is good," Brandon reassured me.

Even though he seemed happy enough to let us take our time getting there, he was enthusiastic about what we'd find and what would happen and how we'd all be reunited when we did arrive in the afterlife. "But seriously," he said through Jamie, "whenever it does happen I'll be so excited to show you what it feels like where I am. Both of you worried about me suffering. I didn't, and I can't wait to prove that to you. Also I'm so excited to show you how beautiful it is here in the afterlife. Also, how easy the transition is when you die."

Brandon makes sure we never forget that he's still alive, whatever it takes to get our attention. Last week when Kenny was in his shop in our garage working, he heard a sharp ting and a ringing sound. The week before he'd hung a crowbar next to a saw on the tool pegboard. Now he turned around, looked up and saw the crowbar swinging back and forth on the pegboard, and realized it had struck the saw blade, creating the ting-ing and ringing. "Yes, Brandon, I'm here." he said out loud. The words just popped out of his mouth without him thinking about them. By now we're so used to Brandon's pranks, those little things that startle us and make us aware that he's still here, we almost take them for granted. Kenny began scolding Brandon affectionately as he often did when he was alive. "What do you *want*?"

I can imagine Brandon thinking, "*Score,* got the old man," throwing his head back and laughing the way he always did. Kenny's gruff scolding voice probably made Brandon laugh even harder.

Chapter 10

Living in the Afterlife

I asked Brandon if he'd be willing to talk a little about what the afterlife was like. He said he was happy to try to describe the afterlife for me. But he also warned me that it might be confusing because the "five senses that you are so used to, to explain the environment, how it smells, how it looks, how it feels" don't necessarily apply there.

On the other hand, during a later meeting with Jamie—my friend Mary was with us that time—Brandon said that in basic ways that don't involve the environment and how you perceive it, the afterlife really isn't that different from this life. Mary asked him whether the afterlife was like an extension of our lives here and not something completely different, and he said that was right. "We still take care of one another, we still have community, we still have purpose, we don't just turn into like clouds or something like that. It's not like we die and become all angelic and all knowing, so much so that we lose personality, that we lose everything we worked so hard to create and all the experiences on earth," he said.

Once I asked him, during an earlier meeting, whether they have things like houses, trees, and grass in the afterlife.

"Yes," he said. "We have trees, we have grass, we have shade, and we have sunshine. We don't necessarily have complete days and nights, cycles or seasons of things. But we do have, let's say, an area that would be winter-like and we have an area that would be summer-like."

And here Brandon said something that seems key to the whole experience of being in the afterlife and how it's different from being in this life: "You can create and manifest any kind of environment that you're interested in."

In the meeting when my friend Mary joined us, I asked him to say more about that. He started off his answer by suggesting that manifesting in his world is as easy as it is for us to think a thought in this world. "People [who are still 'alive'] don't give enough attention to how easy it is to have a thought," he said.

Jamie started laughing and said, "He's showing me an image right now. I won't describe it to you. But I think you can get it if I tell you it's about a body function."

"I'm trying to give you guys a comparison that when you have a thought it happens very easily, that you don't grunt it out like a turd," Brandon explained. "You don't have to heavily focus on it and prep, then squeeze it out of your body. People don't realize how easily energy moves. They just don't give it enough credit. So when we talk about manifesting on this side of the realm, you guys think it's magical or something. But hell, the magic that you guys have on earth is the ease of a thought, that's manifesting. So it's as easy for us to create the things around us, to manifest the realm where we find our creature comforts, as it is for you to have a series of thoughts."

Mary asked Brandon whether it was hard to learn how to manage your thoughts when you first arrived in the afterlife, and whether people in the afterlife ever struggle with manifesting negative thoughts.

"No, that's the weird thing," Brandon said. "That's the thing you have to adjust to almost as soon as you get here. The struggle part that you're mentioning, that's completely human. It's completely human because you guys have the environment to host that vibration. And we don't really have enough [negativity here] to manifest that vibration. So when you go to have a struggling thought or a conflicting thought, it just kind of falls out, it doesn't live, it gets choked out. So we don't end up with the negative thoughts like hate, jealousy, and fear. You could work your ass off and make that happen, but it requires a lot of focus and a lot of work." He added, "It's messed up, but some people do it. To each their own."

Brandon described some examples of environments you'd find in the afterlife that you wouldn't find here. "We have environments that are completely stripped down, comparable to the desert, but imagine just rainbows of colors connected to it."

When I asked him whether the senses were heightened in the afterlife, he said, "It's hard to explain. If I talk about color, you're only going to think about colors [you see] through your eyes. That's not the way we experience color here. We have so many different ways of experiencing color. We have other senses that we can use."

"Do you miss having a body or do you feel like you have a body," I asked him.

"I don't feel like I have a physical body. And I do like it quite a bit. It's less burdensome, there is more freedom with not having a body and there is more ... um..."

"He's trying to find the right word to explain it," Jamie interjected. "I told him to use a thousand words to explain it. Don't let [finding the right word] hold you back."

"Without a physical body," Brandon went on, "there are so many other senses that come along with it. As soon as you get adjusted to a physical body, you're kind of contained in the way you experience others and experience your environment." Brandon/Jamie paused as if Brandon was searching for a way to describe it. "When you're in a physical body, you are zipped up like a piece of luggage. In terms of searching for your spiritual [self] and soul it is so true that your body is the heaviest thing that you carry around on earth.

"We can describe earth easily, because we have these limitations and boundaries. We can look at human life and say okay, when you get to earth you're going to have five senses. You're going to have a day and you're going to have a night. There is a linear expectation. You have those boundaries and you can't get out of it."

"There is no linear time in heaven, right?" I said. Brandon had told me that during another session.

"Right," he said. "So when we look at heaven I can't say to you, 'You will have seven senses when you get here,' because we have this flexibility. There may be sometime when you're only using three of your senses, but there may be sometimes when you are using eight or nine. So how do you describe that? I guess I would say, here everything can exist. We don't have limitations. We can choose the type of knowledge that we want to retain."

"You told Cody that this place fills every crevice of your being. Can you please elaborate?"

"This place fills every crevice of my being," Brandon repeated. "I'm trying to relate it to having a human body and what that would look like, so you can really get the sense of it."

Jamie told me he was showing her that "everything on earth is made up of a mass of particles. Just imagine if you had aware-ness of every particle. It didn't overwhelm you or anything like that. You had an absolute awareness of every particle in your body, and every particle around you. It was very clear, very easy to perceive, no difficulty. That is how I live my life where I am now."

I asked Brandon how he works with physical things in this world. How does he send us dimes, for example? I'd been wondering about this for a while. When I asked him before he always said, rubbing his hands together and clapping, "It's magic!" This time I continued pursuing the question. "How do you make those dimes appear?"

"Oh, it's so much fun! Especially the reaction part, that's my favorite. It's easy once you learn what the dime is made of. You would look at it and you would name the material parts of it, silver, aluminum, this and that. I look at it and see it energetically for what it is, and then I create that."

"Ok, I get it. Well, it is kind of magic."

"You can call it magic," Brandon said, "but when you get here you'll see it's not really magic. It's just a creation. [Everyone here] has the capability of doing creations. We're not playing God or anything. It's just the material mass on earth is so easy to replicate. Once you figure out what it's made of it's easy. It's like making a cake."

I felt surprised by this statement—like making a cake? If it's so easy, I wondered, why don't we see more stuff showing up, coming to us from the spirit world? And then I thought of all the things I'd read about people noticing what seemed like signs from their dead loved ones—butterflies or hummingbirds showing up during family gatherings, flowers growing in odd places, songs playing on the radio that seem to be telling them something—but those people dismissing them or having them dismissed by others.

"I'm not talking about soul and spirit and stuff like that," Brandon went on, saying more about the dimes and how he 'makes' them, and I thought again about how he always says that soul and spirit are what really count and that we have to work on changing our own and making our own lights brighter.

Brandon's comment about seeing what a dime is made of 'energetically' made me realize that everything he's doing is working with things on an energetic level.

I also realized that, from his vantage point in the afterlife, he experiences us in terms of our energy, not our physical bodies. Once he said, "Mom, when you look at people from where I am…You don't just look at their skin and the color of their eyes. You can actually see the undercurrents in a person. Just like the ocean has riptides." He added that this was how he perceived my grief after his death. "You just had this big riptide. It went straight across your heart and kind of flushed all that energy into adrenaline."

I wondered what Brandon himself looked like now. "Would you call yourself a celestial being?" I asked him.

"Mom, what's your definition of celestial being?"

"I suppose something like an angel or a light."

He said, "Everyone has different definitions of an angelic being," and that angels are "pure light energies that have not struggled with earthly dimensions and several other kinds of dimensions as well." Then he put his hands on his hips, according to Jamie, and said, "But that's saying too much."

I asked Brandon whether there were different levels in the spiritual world. "As you learn do you move on to different things?"

"There aren't really levels, like a staircase where you go up and up and up," Brandon said, "or coming in and being really slow and then becoming really fast. But there are awarenesses just like if you were to learn a new task on earth, you wouldn't know how to do it at first, but once you've practiced and experienced it more you can understand it. So that's what I do, I'm ready to learn something, but I don't know how to get there, so I have a teacher who shows up."

Brandon said he'd been learning about unconditional love. In describing that he said something that was intriguing to me because it seemed to show that he is still human even though he lives on the spiritual plane: "Sometimes I have a human mind that jumps in and wants to hold back or reserve [unconditional love]," he said, "and I'm being shown everywhere I go that that's not necessary. I can have my thoughts, my opinion, but I don't need to put them on somebody else. In fact if I try to do that here it doesn't work very well. You kind of look stupid when you do it."

Once when I commented on something irreverent Brandon said in one of my meetings with Jamie, Jamie said he smiled and tilted his head and said, "You can't change." This was also interesting to me because it suggested, once again, that even though Brandon is learning new ways of being in the afterlife, and even though he's in a different world with different fundamentals, he hasn't changed in any essential way, he's still himself. He *can't* change, as he said.

We went back to the subject of him learning new things in the afterlife and how a teacher shows up when he's ready to learn something.

"There are different ones each time," he said, "because you'll find that in spirit if you want to learn about a certain topic, you're going to get a spirit who knows that topic, to come and assist you."

"So you're constantly learning?" I asked.

"Yes, constantly learning," Brandon said. "But it doesn't really give me status or rank or better rank. I learn when I'm ready to understand a concept or the theory."

I took the conversation in a different direction. "Are there certain jobs people do in the afterlife," I asked.

"No," Brandon said. "Here there is nothing that you have to do. We don't have to do something to create an income and some kind of stability. That's just provided to us. Everything that we're expressing or doing for our community or the people around us, it's because we want to. Because when you do [do something for your community because you want to] it creates inner joy, and you become bigger and better. That's the big reward over here. The more joy you spread, the bigger your light becomes."

I nodded, thinking that what Brandon was saying made sense and that it was true here too. That what really matters is positive energy and negative energy and which one you choose, consciously or not, to contribute to any situation. And that the more joy you spread, the bigger your spiritual light becomes.

I found it interesting to hear Brandon use the word community in terms of heaven, and in a later session with Jamie I asked him, "Can you talk about communities in the afterlife? What's your community like? Is it just your relatives, or spirits that you have things or thoughts in common with?"

"Yeah," Brandon answered. "There are communities. We humans are social creatures and we enjoy finding connections through like-minded things. So in the spirit world we enjoy connecting through like-minded emotions. It's not about judgments. We're more interested in whether we feel connected to something. And so we have nature groups here, and we have groups of people who are connected to music."

And then Brandon said something about life in the afterlife that I found totally intriguing. "I would say in general that if you're trying to describe this place, it's closer to the Renaissance period than the Industrial period [of recent history] or the Technology period that we're going through on earth right now, because here we tend to gravitate more towards invention, art, music. We don't need money to survive so manifesting things for a greater purpose, [like in the Industrial age on earth,] doesn't really apply here. We just don't need that in this space. So when we start looking at it through the [eyes of the] era that we're in now on earth, we kind of look a little frou-frou. Because we talk a hell of a lot about music and about community and art and oneness and communication."

I decided to ask him something else I'd been wondering about life in the afterlife—whether he slept. I thought he probably didn't, but I was curious what he'd say about it.

"No, I don't need to," he said simply. "That's only going to slow me down." I laughed, thinking how much like Brandon that was. He never, ever slowed down here either. He was always in high gear, whether he was eating, working, or playing. Nothing was ever in moderation for him. I don't think he knew what the word meant.

Sometimes I try to imagine what Brandon's life is like now. I know it's not really possible to go there but I still like to try. Kenny and I have talked about the afterlife many times and what we always come to is that it's totally vast and incomprehensible. Brandon says it can be anything to anyone, depending on who they are and what they believe. But when it comes down to it, isn't that what this world is like too? My friend Mary says the reason we don't understand or believe in the afterlife is that we don't understand the true nature in this life. We think this world is made of concrete, physical things and that the afterlife can't exist because it's not made of concrete things—it has to be something much more vague. But particle physics tells us there isn't even really a physical world at all and that what we see in this world is all just an illusion created by mechanisms in the brain.

I find that I'm excited to learn more about the afterlife— about that dimension, as Brandon puts it. Not that my journey here is over or that I want it to be over. I'm just curious about what it's like living in the afterlife. And I'm really, really happy that I have a way to talk to Brandon about it, even if he, as he says, can only do his best to help us understand.

Chapter 11

A Body Made of Light

Brandon said he and everyone where he is has a body made of light. He said their bodies resonate in a different dimension, on a different plane, which is why he can walk around us all the time without us seeing him or picking up on him.

When I asked him to say more about his light body during a recent meeting, he joked that his light body was shaped like a hotdog. "Jamie, when you're not looking at me I'm shaped like a hot dog," he said, and then, according to Jamie, he started "cracking up."

Then he got serious and said, "Light body, yes. And within that light body, just like how you have systems for digestion, breathing, living, survival— you know, all those things—we have systems too. Ours are just run through our energetic system, like a light highway and by-way. For you and your human body, what you guys have done is you've trapped your light system inside the physical framework. When we don't have a physical framework we get to have our light body, our light system, work to our benefit in all kinds of ways."

Jamie jumped in: "There's this weird image he's giving me. It's like latitude and longitude light lines and it's moving … zip, zip, zip, really fast. So it looks like a solid light line but it's not, it's like a ball that's running really, really fast."

"Like when you're looking at the fan," Brandon added. "The blades look solid but they're really moving. It's the same principle."

My friend Mary, who was attending the session, asked if the energy he said his light body was made of was something comparable to what people mean when they refer to chakras in our, living bodies.

"Yes," said Brandon through Jamie. "That's the way you've trapped [the light energy] into the physical body. Yeah, Yeah, Yeah.. you got it."

Unlike most of us, Jamie has the ability to see Brandon. This is one of her unusual gifts that makes her who she is. "I see spirit and energy fields the same as I see a person sitting across from me at a table. Sometimes spirit will provide still or moving images within my mind's eye," she says in her book, *With Love and Light.*

I'm not sure what makes it possible for her to see people who are on the other side, but I do know that she describes Brandon exactly as he looked when he was alive on earth, and she described him right from the start. The first time I talked to her she said she saw a young man with short thick dark curly hair and a beautiful smile. She also said he was physically fit and had no mustache. This description captures Brandon perfectly and was one of the things that convinced me Jamie was legitimate. It also made me feel like Brandon really was still alive and that was deeply comforting to me.

That day Jamie also described Brandon sitting, leaning forward with his forearms on both knees and his hands clasped in front of him, which is exactly the way he often sat. When

I asked Brandon what happened—how he died—during that first meeting, Jamie saw him get down on his knees as if he was pleading or begging. Since then Jamie has described Brandon as he has looked, with different expressions and in all sorts of poses, many times. There's something deeply soul satisfying to me to hear him being described in the way that I remember him. Here are some other things Jamie has said, describing him, during our meetings.

When I went to Atlanta for my second appointment with Jamie, in July of 2009, she saw Brandon perched on the arm of the couch with his arm around me. She said Brandon was "very casual." Jamie also commented on the way Brandon acted things out.

In other meetings Jamie has reported him plopping ungracefully down on her couch, wrinkling his nose when he disagrees with what's being said, putting up a finger when he's trying to make a point, putting up his fingers and making air quotes when he's trying to get a point across, taking a bow or patting himself on the back when we're talking about something he had a hand in like the dolphins at Cody's wedding, making jokes and laughing really hard, standing up and walking around when he's excited about something. "He doesn't sit still very well," Jamie commented. He also raises his voice when he feels strongly about something. "Wow, he's really getting loud," Jamie said once, when Brandon was talking about how some accident deaths are mislabeled as suicide, as his was by the police.

Once, when I asked him, "Do you have anything to say to Dad?" Jamie said, "He's pretending to reach in his back pocket and pull out a long sheet of paper." He did the same thing during another meeting when I asked him if he had anything to say to Jessica. He rubbed his hands together and said, "It's magic," when I asked him how he could make all those dimes appear in all those weird and unusual places. He cuts his eyes over at Jamie and repeats himself for emphasis when he wants to poke a little fun at me.

Anyone who knew Brandon on this earth will recognize him in these gestures. I hate it that Brandon no longer has a physical body that I can hug and see and touch, even though he has said through Jamie that he likes not having a physical body "quite a lot." But hearing Jamie describe his actions and gestures as he talks to me through her gives me a reassuring sense that his spirit is definitely still around, and that in a way, maybe, the spirit *is* the body, and that can never be destroyed.

CHAPTER 12

BRANDON ON DYING AND DEATH

Brandon always says that death doesn't hurt, it isn't a big deal, and we should all stop worrying about it. "The only thing [death] gets rid of is your physical body. That's it. Boom," he said one day through Jamie.

Recently I asked him again what happened when he first passed. I remembered what he told me the first time I met with Jamie—how he was fooling around with a gun at his friend's house, heard a loud bang, threw the gun down on the floor, and then realized he wasn't in his body any more. But I had a few more questions. He'd said then that after he figured out he couldn't get back in his body, he looked around and saw a woman standing behind him. "Who are you?" he said and she said, "Come with me." It turned out she was Henrietta Eilander, his great-grandmother, my father's mother, who died in Newton, Iowa, in 1946. Her death was caused by a tiny injury—she punctured her finger with a sewing needle—and the wound became septic and she died of blood poisoning.

I was surprised to hear that Henrietta was there when Brandon passed. I'd always thought that if I or any of us died we'd be met by my dad, who passed in 1979 and to whom I was very close. I was born in 1956 and had never met Henrietta, and Brandon certainly wasn't anywhere near the age where he could have met her—he never even saw a picture of her.

In my recent meeting with Jamie I asked Brandon why Henrietta met him instead of somebody else. "Is there a particular family member who's designated to meet someone when they pass?" I asked.

"Well, it's not like first come, first serve," Brandon said through Jamie, "and it's definitely not set up as, this person is your job, and this person is your job. It has more purpose to it. I'm talking about the talent of the person, the personality matches, the fact that someone can get through to a [particular person who passes]. What the human relationship was. Because you know sometimes…if there was something painful between you and a family member who died before you, most likely that person is not going to be there for you [when you pass] even though he's already healed and everything is fine."

My friend Mary, who was there during that meeting too, came back to the idea that someone meets you whose personality matches yours. She pointed out that that didn't seem to be the case with Henrietta.

Brandon agreed. "Yeah, I don't feel that way for her." He went on to explain why Henrietta was a good "greeter" for him. "She could talk plain to me. She was very forward, she could be like a brick house. I needed that awakening to be able to understand where I was and what was going on. And there weren't that many people I loved who were in spirit." He said his pets were who he would have wanted most to see in the afterlife, and I realized that was probably true—he was too young when he died to know many people who had already passed. (In a later meeting Brandon confirmed that there are animals, including our pets who have passed, in the afterlife.)

Returning to the subject of why Henrietta greeted him, he said, "For me, I needed more technical assistance, not so much the emotional support."

I reminded him that Henrietta had had seven children so she had plenty of experience telling young people what to do, and Brandon said, "Oh, she's got experience and she'll sit and tell you and she'll talk to you forever about it."

Mary asked him if Henrietta was still with him all the time like she was in the beginning. ("I can't get rid of her," Brandon said during my first meeting with Jamie.) "I get some free time now. Especially now I tell her I'm an author, my mom is on top of things. She lets me be," he said, and we all laughed.

Brandon said once that "a lot of people here see their death day as a day of celebration, sort of like a graduation," although, he said, he didn't look at his that way. I was interested in the idea of a "death day" and particularly struck by the thought that many people on the other side celebrate it like a graduation. This idea contrasts starkly with what most people on this side feel about the anniversary of their loved one's passing, which seems like a dark day not only for them but for the person who died. In the early years that was certainly true for us—the anniversary of Brandon's death was horrible for us. But these days we choose to have fun on the anniversary, to celebrate his life instead of mourn his death, because we know that's what he wants. And because he himself is obviously still not far away, vibrantly alive, and part of our lives.

I asked Brandon if people who pass tend to stay very close to this part of the realm in the beginning. "For example," I asked, "do they go to their own funerals?"

"Most of us choose to kind of hang out and watch the funeral," Brandon confirmed. "There's something about having that all zipped up. And there's something about recognizing that, you know, it's real." Brandon's further explanation about why it was desirable for dead people to go to their own funerals seemed to suggest that otherwise they might not come to grips with the fact of their own deaths or be able to relate to the shock and grief of their survivors.

"When you die you want [everything] to be the same as it was [when you were alive]. But it's not going to be like that because [your loved ones] have had the experience of the funeral. If we [dead people] don't have the experience of the funeral, we're kind of picking up where we left off and you're not. You guys have moved on."

What he was saying struck me as very similar to why we 'humans' need to hold funerals and sometimes even view the body, so we can get closure and begin to let go of denial. I barely remember Brandon's funeral because I was so distraught during it. But I do believe firmly, and I knew even at the time, that Brandon's body was just a vessel— it wasn't him in that casket—and that he was still with us somehow. Still, I miss that vessel desperately and it's that missing that's still hard for me. I have many pictures of Brandon

Brandon Smith
1980-2008

Brandon
smiling for
the camera.

The kids having their picture taken at the five and dime store.

Brandon, Cody, and Jessica the summer before Brandon passed.

Brandon and Jessica in our local
4th of July parade in 1984.

Father and son.
This was taken
when Brandon
was about a
year old.

Two-year-old
Brandon at
Christmas with
his very first
baseball cap and
glove

Brandon communing with Santa.

Brandon mugs for camera while Jessica holds Cody, their new baby brother.

Brandon and Cody, ages nine and five, very happy with their baseball cards.

Brandon turning ten on June 10th at Wrigley Field, with his best friend Bill and Uncle David. This was probably the best day of Brandon's life.

Brandon sleeping on my lap at the kitchen table.

Brandon and Kenny celebrating after pheasant hunting.

Brandon and his mom (me) in a restaurant in Iowa City.

Brandon wearing his new Christmas present. This was taken in 2000 when he was twenty.

Brotherly love. Brandon and Cody celebrating in 2006.

Brandon talking to Grandpa Smith at a wedding, the summer before Brandon passed.

This was taken the day all the men in Kenny's family reroofed Grandpa Smith's house. Grandpa Smith chose Brandon to be in charge.

Brandon in October 2007.

Dolphins that showed up beside the boat at Cody's wedding.

Lesa on vacation in Florida five years after Brandon passed. Note the mysterious orb that shows up in this and other photos.

and I love to look at them. Photos do capture who he was and is, in some mysterious way.

Mary asked one more question about newly passed people attending their own funerals. "It seems like you're saying that where you are is where you put your attention. You can put your attention on the funeral and that's where you are, right?"

"Yes!" Brandon said.

∿

Brandon had said during an earlier meeting that he's aware of it every time someone in this world thinks about him. During our recent meeting Mary asked him what that was like, whether he was bombarded all the time with people thinking about him, and he said, "At the beginning, you would absolutely say yes, because you have no concept of how to organize what's coming at you. So it's a little bit like, 'How can I run from this? How can I turn this off?' It's like watching a movie you really don't want to watch. Or being on a roller coaster ride that you don't really want to be on but it just keeps going."

He described what happens when someone here thinks about him like this: "It's a feeling. You get it right in your entire body." (I thought this was interesting: What body? He refers to having a light body in the next sentence.) "And the placement of where it shows up in your light body," he went on, "is dependent on what kind of emotion is attached to that memory or to that thought or that prayer.

Even just the thought of me goes right to me. I think that's why people like Mom, when they lose someone they love, feel like they have to think about them all the time to keep them alive. I really think that's where that comes from and that's where it translates."

I said I remembered doing that right after Brandon passed—I felt like if I didn't keep him in my thoughts all the time I'd lose him. I might have been feeling like that, Brandon seemed to be suggesting, because unconsciously I *was* connecting with him through my thoughts even though I didn't know I was, and I didn't want to lose that connection. "But you and I know that's not true now [that I would lose my connection with you if I wasn't thinking about you], Brandon," I said when we were talking about this in the meeting with Jamie.

"But the masses don't," Brandon said.

I asked Brandon to talk a little bit more about relationships between people who are on his side of the realm (dead people, although, as Brandon would say, they're not dead) and those of us here.

"We still have the [same] relationships with each other," he said. "It's not like death severs anything. Everything that we've cultivated and built is still continuing—all the emotional connections that we had with people. All of that continues after life."

My friend Mary pointed out that many people who are still here in this part of the realm (those of us who are still 'alive') don't believe their dead loved ones are anywhere at all, let alone believe in the possibility of having an on-going relationship with them.

"Right. Right," Brandon said. "That kind of feeds to the work that we get to do beyond, in this place. Beyond earth."

When Mary asked him, "How so?" he said, "Well, because here we're still playing out those relationships but the people on earth are not involved in the same way, because they're not seeing us in our dead presence and being able to communicate with us [like we're doing now using Jamie as a medium]. Carrying on the relationship is what we're doing on our end and it kind of becomes a little bit of our work."

"What do you mean, you're doing it on your end? What are you doing?"

"Energetically, we hold onto those characteristics that we had when we were alive. So if [for example] there was bickering over who made coffee the best, every time someone alive goes to make a cup of coffee, they remember that, they get [sent back to that happening with the person who passed] in that moment. And the person who passed is contributing to that memory of bickering.

"When you say, "Oh I wish so and so was here," you're probably saying that because so and so *is* here. You guys think your brain is running the show but it's more your brain picking up signals. Most people think that all memories are just brain recall. They think the memory was stored [in the brain] and they're going back to the library and bringing it up. But that's not true. Most of those memories pop up because your dead person is there [with you] and they're going, 'You-hoo...remember that memory?' That's how they're continuing to play out that relationship, the bickering over the coffee.

And they're also sending you support to have courage, giving you an embrace when you're down."

"Can you say something about how you perceive us here in this world?" I asked Brandon. "What do you 'see'? Do you see us all the time, do you see me all the time or only when you visit?

"I can see you all the time if I want."

I, of course, can't see him, but I like to think of him being in the room with me, at least mostly—sometimes it seems a little strange to think of him watching me when I can't watch him. Mostly, I'm thrilled to know he's around—to still have any relationship with him at all. And when I think of all the people who've lost someone, who don't have what I have with Brandon—who don't even have an inkling that their lost loved ones are still alive and nearby—I feel a sense of urgency to tell them this: You can find and continue to carry on a relationship with your son or your husband or your father or daughter or whoever it is that you love who's on the other side. And when you do find them and reach out and begin to talk to them it will bring you enormous joy and peace.

Chapter 13

Still Part of the Family

At Christmastime a few years ago, Kenny and I met with Jamie—and Brandon—a few days before the holiday. Jamie started out the meeting by saying, "Brandon's looking forward to the holidays. He's really excited because he gets to go back and forth [between houses] and see everyone. He can go wherever he wants to go."

"I'm going to be around for the holidays," Brandon confirmed, "and I'm going to leave you some signs."

I smiled. Even though talking to Brandon through Jamie had eased my grief a lot by then—this was 2013 and Brandon died in 2008—the holidays were still really hard for me. But hearing Brandon say he'd be with us for Christmas made me feel better, and after that meeting I put up our Christmas tree for the first time since Brandon passed. He was the last one to take it down, seven days before he died. It's funny—I've tried to give that tree away many times since Brandon left us, to friends, family members, even Goodwill, but nobody can or will take it. Now I'm glad we kept it. It's a beautiful tree and whenever I put it up I think of Brandon. Sometimes I still cry a little and feel sad, but then something will happen – someone will call and say, "You wouldn't believe where I found a dime," or tell me about some other sign they got from Brandon, reminding us that he's still here—and I'll smile and feel better.

"Don't think you're all alone in this," Brandon said, that day in 2013 right before Christmas, and I remembered once again that even though we can't see him or talk to him in the normal way, Brandon is still with us.

I've come to believe that my little grandchildren—Cody's daughter McKinli, who's three this year, and his son Calvin, who was born seven years after Brandon passed—have more sense of Brandon's presence in the room than I or most adults do. In my meetings with Jamie Brandon confirms that McKinli and Calvin do interact with him. He tells me he rolls around on the floor with them and loves to make them laugh hard, and that because of their innocence they're "enlightened." I believe it—children are so open and innocent and they came here not very long ago from the place Brandon lives now. I imagine they take it all in willingly and accept the presence of a loved one's spirit without hesitation. I love to think about Brandon visiting them and finding ways to delight them. He comforts them too—once he told me that when McKinli wakes up at night and is scared in her crib he pats her back until she goes back to sleep. (Sometimes McKinli says in her little girl voice, "Pat my back, please," and Britni and Cody themselves have started getting her back to sleep that way.) Brandon often says he loves McKinli and Calvin as much as he would if they were his own children.

One day about two years ago, Britni told me over the phone about something that had just happened. McKinli was cutting teeth at the time. She was sitting in her high chair and Britni was trying to open a package of teething tablets to help her gums feel better. Britni said that when she was struggling mightily to take the plastic off the top of the bottle McKinli started belly-laughing. She gave a big loud laugh three or four times as Britni kept not being able to get the bottle open. Britni said it was strange for McKinli to find what she was doing so funny. It seemed unusual to me too, and Britni and I agreed Brandon probably had a hand in it. I could just picture him standing there next to McKinli's high chair making faces, laughing, and pointing at Britni.

Brandon told me once through Jamie that he tried to explain to McKinli that he comes to visit her but lives in a different place. McKinli seems to have absorbed this message. Once, when she and her mother were going to visit her cousins, who'd come from Colorado to see Britni's parents in Des Moines for Christmas, she was reciting the names of all her cousins, aunts, and uncles who would be there that day at her grandparents house—and at the end she added "and Brandon." Britni called me on her cell phone as soon as McKinli said that. She was laughing when I picked up the phone. She told me the story and said, "Evidently Brandon's coming to our family's house for Christmas."

McKinli certainly acts as if she knows Brandon. When she walks by his picture hanging on the wall in our living room she waves at it and says, "Hi, Brandon."

There have been a few times when Kenny and I noticed McKinli acting like she saw Brandon in the room. Once when we had her for the weekend when she was about one and a half years old, we were sitting in the living room drinking our coffee early one morning when she toddled across the room blowing kisses into the air behind the couch. "Look at her," I said to Kenny. He agreed she must've been blowing kisses to her uncle.

That couch was the spot where Brandon always hung out when he was in the house—he napped there, watched football games and Planet Earth and Seinfeld there, lay there with his head on a pillow and read novels and autobiographies and books about history. I've noticed that when we sense his presence in the house he usually shows up in the spots where he spent the most time when he was alive. Another place I often feel him around me is in the kitchen. When he was alive he loved to hang out with me there, sitting at the breakfast bar telling me one of his long detailed stories. (His fifth-grade teacher told his grandma that he needed to be a writer, and she used the work he did in those long-ago classes as examples of how to write a short story or a poem for her students until she retired a few years ago.)

On the day after he died and during the rest of that week, the door of his old bedroom in our basement kept opening on its own. I must've shut it at least twenty-five times, and every time I went back down there it was open again. Sometimes I still sense his presence when I'm in that room. And sometimes, I swear, I can almost hear the sound of his boots on the stairs. He lived with us for about a year after he graduated from college, before he bought his own small one-bedroom house on the other side of the lake, and every morning at five o'clock he woke up Kenny and me climbing the stairs from his basement bedroom, wearing his heavy work boots, on his way to his job in construction. He sounded like an elephant coming up the stairs. I really do miss that part.

∾

Brandon tells me that he stays very busy watching over our family, and I can think of at least one example where I believe he headed off something really bad. About two years ago, Grandpa and Grandma Smith, Kenny's parents, were driving on a two-lane highway in rural Iowa when Grandpa Smith's heart went out of rhythm and then completely stopped. His pacemaker/defibrillator kicked in and restarted his heart, but before that happened he slumped over the wheel and lost control of the car, the car went into the ditch and ended up in the middle of a cornfield. (I can only imagine how terrifying this would have been for Kenny's mom. She was upset for months afterwards.)

This episode came up during Kenny's and my meeting with Brandon in December 2013. Kenny had been worrying about his dad ever since the accident and was probably looking for reassurance from Brandon, who'd always been close to Grandpa Smith. Brandon had been a golden child who could do no wrong in Grandpa and Grandma Smith's eyes.

"Grandpa's doing great… at least we aren't finding him in a ditch," Brandon said in the meeting with Jamie.

"Was he in a ditch?" Jamie asked.

I told Jamie about how Grandpa and Grandma Smith ended up in the middle of a cornfield after Grandpa drove off the road. "You must have been with them, Brandon," I said. "I have no idea how it came to be that they didn't hit a post or pole."

"Man, I did everything I could do to make sure they missed every kind of obstacle possible," Brandon said. "They just kind of drove right off into the ditch."

Looking through my transcripts of my meetings with Jamie, I still find this particular conversation with Brandon amazing. Clearly, it's Brandon talking. I can almost hear his voice aloud in his words—"I've been taking bets he wouldn't know how to retire," and "Man, I did everything I could." And there's absolutely no way Jamie could have known about Grandpa Smith's accident; we only told her more about it after Brandon brought it up.

Brandon consistently finds ways to remind us of his presence during important family occasions. There were the dolphins leaping and whirling and twirling in the water around our two boats at Cody's wedding, which Brandon confirmed he had orchestrated during Cody's first session with Jamie. "I'm not going to miss this one [either]," Brandon said when I met with Jamie a few days before Jessica's wedding on May 1st, 2015. Jamie said that he was showing her images of himself dropping a fist-full of dimes to the floor. Brandon also talked in that session about how he planned to protect Jessica and her new husband as they embarked on their life together.

Jessica's wedding was held on Turks and Caicos, a small British island in the Caribbean. The day after the wedding the bride and groom and some of Jessica's friends took a daytime boating trip around the island. As a regular part of the excursion, the boat captain always dives off the side of the boat and brings up two or three conch shells. On one of his dives that day, he found an intact sand dollar on the ocean floor. He presented it to Jessica because she was the bride, although another passenger on the boat really wanted it. Jessica showed it to me and Kenny when she came back from the boating excursion. "I know this came from Brandon. It's my wedding gift from him," she said, and all we could do was nod and wipe the tears from our eyes. Jessica brought the sand dollar home, carefully wrapped in tissue paper in her suitcase, and she still has it, prominently displayed on a shelf in her living room. When we were reading about sand dollars recently we were even more struck by the meaning of the sand dollar as a gift to Jessica on her wedding day. Originally, when she was planning her wedding back 2014, she decided she wanted to release doves after the ceremony as a way to commemorate Brandon and her new husband Chris's mother's deaths. But it turned out the government of Turks and Caicos wouldn't let her bring doves to the island, so that part of the wedding plan had to be scratched. When we were researching sand dollars recently we learned that when you break a sand dollar open, five dove-shaped parts come out—five little white doves. According to legend, the five white doves in the sand dollar are symbols of good will and peace.

We're on the brink of another set of holidays as I write this. This year I feel even more confident that Brandon will be with us during the sometimes-difficult holiday season. I'm clearer than ever about the fact that he's still part of our family and always will be, not just as a set of memories but as a living, active participant. And I know that if I ever start doubting that, he'll be sure to remind me.

Chapter 14

Spiritual Lessons

Brandon is extremely excited about communicating the spiritual lessons he's learned since he's been living in the afterlife. Over the last eight plus years I've been blessed to learn many things about life and death from him.

Brandon's death itself, aside from what Brandon has taught me through Jamie, has been a kind of spiritual healing for me, even though I would never have asked to heal that way or have wanted to believe something good could come of Brandon's passing. Brandon addressed this when he said one day through Jamie, "Even though [my dying] was a huge kick in the face [to you], you learned over the years how to deal with that and redefined yourself. It gave you a voice to share with others. There was a great leap of faith and knowledge [that came] with all of this."

When I asked him, during a meeting with Jamie five years ago, "How do you think I'm doing as far as my spiritual and whole mental well being goes?" Brandon said, "Finally you are out of the black hole. You're not going back there. Oh, it has been a struggle. It was so hard [for us here] because we were looking at you and you were Mom, but everything inside of you wasn't. It was really hard. Mom, really what brought you out of the hole, you did it yourself. Everyone tried to throw you a rope and rescue you, but you really weren't reaching out for anyone. It was just kind of your way of suffering. Your way of grieving. What keeps you out of the hole is your knowledge and awareness."

Brandon described how he perceived my grieving process. "There was no way you could control or ground yourself. No way for anyone, not even me, to give you direction. I tried to help you a little bit here and there but mostly I had to just step back and let you do it. I finally know what it is like to be a parent!"

Brandon began talking about how we all need to let each other feel however we're feeling. "People think grief or sadness are bad emotions. If you're in possession of sadness, they think, then you're less than, not complete or whole. It's all bullshit. It would be so great if we could just pony up and honor how every other person wants to think, feel or do. It will be so great when we start worshipping individuality, instead of feeling like a bunch of sheep in a herd."

During the same session Brandon said to me, "During these last three weeks you've been more confident in handling whatever comes to you that day." I had just started going to a new grief counselor at that point and it was true, I was feeling stronger.

Kenny was going to the grief counselor with me and Brandon commented on that too. "I'm happy Dad is going to the grief counselor with you. If you didn't make those changes, the two of you were heading toward divorce. That was the only option available. You didn't know how to turn your ship around and he never wanted to be on the ship so it created a bit of a void."

Working on ourselves and our relationship has been one of the biggest spiritual gifts Kenny and I have received since

Brandon died. No one understands the hurt and pain of losing a child like we do. It's hard to describe it to anyone else, even to our other children, and we've learned how to lean on each other, protect each other, and communicate deeply with each other in a way that has enriched our marriage.

Even though I was always open to life after death, I've stretched my spiritual beliefs a lot since I've been talking to Brandon. This probably holds even more true for Kenny. Kenny and I agreed that the message Brandon has given us regarding death and dying is probably the message that has touched us most deeply. Brandon always uses the same phrases over and over: Dying is like being born, it doesn't hurt, don't worry yourself about death, it's a transition, it's *coming home.*

These messages, and the fact that Brandon is clearly talking to us and is therefore still alive, has given us the freedom to put the fear of death behind us and look at it from an entirely new perspective. Losing the fear of death and dying has been a gift that has soothed our souls greatly. It feels as if we've been set free from a burden.

Fear in general is another thing Kenny and I discussed when we were talking about what we've learned from Brandon. We humans are taught to be afraid of all kinds of threats from the time we're small children, and while we do need to learn rules like "look both ways before you cross the street," we're often given the message by our parents, who were given it to them by their parents and by the culture at large, that life isn't safe. From talking to Brandon and Jamie many times, I've come to believe on a deep level that life actually is safe, and that there's truly nothing to fear but fear itself. This is something I keep having to learn over and over to overcome my old conditioning, and that I probably always will have to keep learning.

I've lost the fear of many things since Brandon's been gone: My fear of death, my fear of what others think of me, my fear of things I have no control over—in earlier years I told my boys they could never even own a motorcycle, but nowadays my daughter rides on the back of her husband's motorcycle all the time and I don't even give it a second thought, because I know I have no control over what happens and I've given what happens over to God. I'm not perfect now at letting go of things I can't change, but I'm a lot better than I used to be: I used to think I had control over everything in my life and that I could prevent bad things from happening. Now I know that we're not writing the story of our lives and we have very little to say about our own destiny.

Brandon always encourages me to *live in the now.* I used to be so caught up in all the things I had to do in everyday life that it was hard for me to take time to appreciate each day and be thankful for what I had. Now I go for long walks and spend time sitting on my porch looking out at the lake. I pray and meditate and count my blessings. I try to be present in every moment instead of going through the motions while focusing on my thoughts and worries.

Brandon is constantly trying to teach me that awareness, not ignorance, is bliss. He doesn't want me to dwell on the bad things that have happened in my life, but he wants me to address them instead of avoiding them. It's easy to ignore bad things and hope they'll go away, but, I've learned, they won't go away. I've found this to be particularly true of grief, which I believe will find you no matter how hard you try to avoid it. If you try to hide from it with alcohol or drugs or non-stop TV-watching or simply by ignoring it, it will fester inside and possibly even destroy you. I also think that when Brandon tells me that awareness, not ignorance, is bliss, he's trying to make sure I keep an open mind and heart and continue to grow and communicate with him.

Learning how to ask for help and address my feelings have been two other important of gifts I've received since Brandon died. At first, after he passed, I kept all my feelings inside and tried to become my own counselor, which didn't work. On the outside I was still Mom but on the inside I shut down. Everyone tried to throw me a rope or a lifeline, but I had to do the work myself. Brandon talked about all this during some of my early meetings with Jamie. "[My passing] gave you an awareness that you don't have to know everything or have all the answers and now can be your new 'normal,'" he said once.

With the passing of time, and with the positive perspective I've acquired from meeting with Jamie and talking to Brandon, I've come to appreciate life and living more than ever before. I've gotten increased respect for myself and my own strength and resilience. And I now have the ability to empathize with others as a result of my own experience of loss.

One day in a meeting with Jamie I asked Brandon what he thought my spiritual gifts were, and he said right away, "Being a mom. Being a grandma. I totally see it in a new light now. Those are spiritual gifts. I want you to understand that the mom role really uses [your spiritual] gifts." I believe Brandon was saying that I haven't really valued what I do as a mother and a grandmother. It hasn't felt like work—it's something I've done purely out of love without even really thinking about it. But I've devoted a good part of my life to it and if I don't stop and think about it, it's easy to feel like I haven't been contributing anything real in terms of work. Brandon was telling me that I should realize that what I've contributed *is* important and that I should feel good about it.

I do know this on one level, but on another level it's still something I have to keep learning over and over. Since Brandon's death I've changed the way I look at myself and what I do in the world. I still believe that the most important things in life are your relationships—with your children, your husband, with whoever's important in your life—but now I'm focusing more on myself and my own lessons and my own journey. When I was a mom I was so busy I didn't even have time to think about myself and I put everyone's needs before my own. That's what you do when you're a mother and a wife. But now I realize that you need to put yourself first, at least a little, in order to have something to give to others; if you do nothing but give yourself away you'll have nothing left.

I've also realized, since Brandon died, that my identity was all wrapped up in what happened to him and my other kids. When Brandon died I buried a big part of myself along with his body. I felt like I had spent all this energy helping him become the person he was, and now all that was for nothing because he was gone. But now I know that he's not gone. And not only that, he tells me that what I gave him as a mother was exactly what he needed, and it was all he needed: He doesn't regret not marrying or having children, because he got all the love he needed from me and the rest of his family. I felt deeply satisfied when he said that, and it made me feel like I had done my job as his mother, that I had put forth every effort I could to help him become the person he was, and it did matter—a lot.

Brandon and I also talked, during that session, about other spiritual gifts I have, such as intuition and the ability to tell the difference between positive and negative energies. "You being more sensitive, that came to you naturally, I think you always had that. [Dad and I] didn't feel things or translate things the way you did."

Brandon proceeded to describe some tendencies of mine that are probably common to many people who have what's usually referred to as codependency. He gave me some suggestions that I believe would be helpful to anyone. "When you feel an emotion, I would like it if you would just ask yourself, is that mine? Is this something I created or is this something I'm just picking up from someone else? Your head is so used to just saying that whatever you're feeling belongs to you, and that's not always the truth. Mom, I've seen it, you can pick up on the sorrow of the person next to you and be sad as all get out yourself for the rest of the day for no reason. It's amazing. But if you just ask yourself, is that [emotion] mine and the answer is no, then I want you to say, 'Well, whose is it?'"

Brandon described how to figure out whose emotions and energy I was picking up, if I wasn't feeling my own: "You'll look around the room and you'll lock on someone and you won't want to let go. That's when you'll know you're mimicking that person's energy pattern. [You're doing it unconsciously] so you can gain information about how they're feeling and what they're going through. That's all your body wants to do is constantly give you information." Brandon said my tendency to take on other people's energy and moods was exhausting for me. Nevertheless, despite the pitfalls and challenges of being so sensitive, my ability to be aware of other people's energy was a gift, he said. "That *knowing* that you have, that is what is going to grow," he said.

I do feel like my intuition and my "knowing," as Brandon calls it, have grown since he's passed and I've been talking to him. Mostly I've come to trust them more. I've found that when I'm in a group of people I can sense who's going to drain my energy if I talk to them and who's going to give me more energy, and I tend to gravitate toward the latter and avoid the former.

Brandon commented once on the lessons he himself has learned from his own death – mostly from what caused his death. Our meeting that day fell on the day before the sixth anniversary of his passing so his passing was on all of our minds. "[My death] needs to be like an ode to making mistakes," he said. Jamie said he wrinkled his nose when he said that. "That's really what I see on my death day. Is looking at my mistakes. How could I have been more aware, how could I have been less careless? It would be really great if our family would take that on as a tradition, if they would look at their lives on my death day and see how they could pay more attention and be more careful."

In a recent meeting with Jamie, Brandon and I came back

to how he's been learning about unconditional love in the afterlife. He told me a spirit, Holly, had been helping him.

"She's been real good about it, she talks pretty much straight up with me," he said. "She shows me that I can have my own internal thoughts, but it doesn't have to jeopardize how I'm interacting with somebody else. You know, I never learned that on earth. I was the whole package, I wasn't going to hold something back, I was just going to be me no matter what. But now what I'm learning is that being your true, vulnerable self and being completely open is actually showing your soul more and that's being more truthful. So I can have my opinions, I can carry them with me, but really what I present is how I feel, not what I think. If somebody wants my opinion, they can ask me for it and I can give it to them, but if I hand it over right away it doesn't help the situation. That all kind of wraps up under unconditional love. Now that I know what unconditional love is, I'm totally fine with experiencing it and putting it out there."

Jamie tells me that the light around Brandon when we have our readings is larger than it was when we started, which doesn't surprise me. I'm amazed by all the ways Brandon has grown and changed on the other side. His being on the other side has opened my mind and spirit too, probably almost as much as his. When I think about it I feel like we've risen to the occasion together, and that the occasion has turned out to be a continual joint effort involving enlarging our spiritual learning and light—his light, my light, our two lights together. I know that he is a part of me that will never leave me, and that this new stage in our relationship is just part of our journey together.

CHAPTER 15

COMMUNICATIONS FROM BEYOND

Jamie has commented on the fact that Brandon seems to be extremely good at communicating. It makes sense that Brandon would approach communicating from beyond with such enthusiasm, determination, and persistence, because when he was in this life he took great pleasure in talking—a lot, enthusiastically, with a grin on his face—to anyone he liked, which was just about everyone. He told long, funny, somewhat tedious stories—about how he got stuck in the mud and tried to get help from the guy down the road who kept people off his property with a rifle, how he dropped his wallet in the lake when he was fishing and found it with a magnet and a pole, how he rescued a stuffed monkey from a dumpster, stuck it onto his back using its velcro hands, and wore in into the construction site where he was working saying, 'I can't get this monkey off my back!' I can still picture the way he would tell those stories, going into lots of detail, going on and on, because he wanted to make sure you felt as if you were there, almost as if you were a part of the story yourself. And now he's found a way, more than one way, to communicate from the other side.

It's not just me he talks to either. Once, when I called Jamie for my meeting, she said, "Guess who showed up early? Brandon showed up in my office at about 6:50 a.m., and I saw him standing there laughing, so I ran to my calendar and checked who I was talking with first."

She said she told her office mate, "I get to talk to the coolest person now. If you don't believe in any of this you need to talk to him, because he lays it out in a way you feel like, there's no way [this isn't real]. He blows me out of the water by how smart and witty he is."

I felt so proud when I heard her say all that, and Brandon did too. "He loves that I'm talking about him right now, "Jamie said.

At that moment in the meeting she reported that Brandon said, "Dwan! Dwan!" Dwan was a nickname I used to call Brandon sometimes, and when I heard it coming out of Jamie's mouth the hair on my arms stood on end.

When Brandon wants to get a message to me and I don't have a meeting with Jamie coming up, he will go to great lengths to communicate in some other way. There was that time in 2010 when he inserted himself into his friend Miranda's dream and insisted that she tell me and Kenny not to sell our house. Another stunning example happened in the fall of 2013.

My friend Donella, who lives in New Zealand, sees a medium there about every six months. During her appointment in October 2013, the medium was talking to Donella about her life and then suddenly stopped. "Do you have a close friend who lost a son?" she asked.

"Yes," Donella said.

"Your friend's son is sending me an urgent message. He's saying he won't go away until I pass it on to you. Here it is:

You need to call your friend immediately and relay the message that his death was definitely an accident." Then the medium asked Donella, "How did he die?"

"He died from a gunshot wound," Donella said.

"You must contact her immediately and let her know," the medium told her again.

Donella phoned me and relayed the message as soon as she got out of her reading with the medium.

I had been meeting with Jamie for four years by then and I had already received the message from Brandon that his death was an accident. But at the time that Brandon broke into Donella's meeting with the psychic, I was going through the DCI report about Brandon's death, including the autopsy. I'd glanced at them both back in the beginning of 2009 but I'd had to put them away then, and now I was going through them carefully, sentence by sentence, trying to figure out what happened, and I was in a very dark place. Even though Brandon had told me himself through Jamie that he had shot himself by accident and it had nothing to do with being depressed or wanting to die, I was questioning that again and also questioning myself, wondering if I should have or could have done something to prevent him from shooting himself.

Donella had no idea what I was doing at the time or what kind of state I was in. "What's going on?" she said when she called me. And then she told me about how Brandon broke into her appointment with her medium and insisted that she, Donella, call me and tell me his death was an accident.

I told her what was happening to me and how much I had

needed to hear—to be reminded of—what Brandon was telling me: His death was an accident. It wasn't my fault. He didn't do it on purpose.

Donella and I were both amazed at Brandon's persistence and determination to get that message to me. It was October and I didn't have a meeting scheduled with Jamie until December.

When I think of this story now, I'm even more amazed than I was when I was in the middle of my dark ruminations and didn't have much distance on anything. Once Donella passed Brandon's message on I started to feel better.

Donella and I talked about that afterwards, for at least a year—how Brandon managed to use her and her medium to get that message to me. Then, about two months ago, Brandon showed up again when Donella went to see her medium. This time Donella asked her medium at the beginning of the session if Brandon was present. The medium said no and they proceeded with their in-person meeting. All of a sudden, about halfway through, the medium stopped talking.

Donella called me the next day and told me what happened. "Brandon showed up for just for a minute. He wanted to thank [my medium] for getting his earlier message to you. That's all he said and then he left. My medium was crying when she told me," Donella said. "I've never seen her cry before. She kept saying how sweet it was of Brandon to come to her and say thank you."

Of course I took full credit and wanted affirmation. "See?" I said. "I did raise him right, didn't I?" thinking it would be just like Brandon to do something like that.

The more I communicate with Brandon the better it gets. In the beginning when I started meeting with Jamie, I found it overwhelming. I desperately wanted to talk to Brandon but I was so emotional during the meetings it was hard to focus on what I was hearing. I kept having to try not to cry all the time. And I didn't exactly feel comfortable with the process. I had never done anything like it before and at that time I think I was still holding onto some skepticism.

I was also very aware of, and somewhat influenced by, the fact that other people would probably be skeptical about what I was doing. I was right to be aware of other people's likely skepticism. Brandon once said to me when I was talking to Jamie, "Mom, don't pull out your pendulum and say, 'Just a minute, let me ask my dead son,' in front of people. They'll think you've lost it."

I kept worrying about how I would explain my communication with Brandon to other people. I knew it was Brandon talking through Jamie, but I wondered how in the world I was going to convince other people of that.

Brandon tried to help me. "Remember, Mom, when people use the word crazy they also used to believe the world was flat," Brandon said, addressing my fear that people would think I was crazy for thinking I was talking to him. He said everyone had to go through their own personal evolution in terms of believing in the afterlife, and that I had a "step up" on many people because of what I'd been through. "Your eyes have been opened, so to speak," he said. "It's [always] difficult leading the way. You check things out and try to prove to others that what you're experiencing is true. The faith in this afterlife communication comes in two steps. Number one: You start to believe in it yourself. Number two: You believe in it enough that you don't need your environment's approval."

I finally decided it didn't matter what other people thought of my communication with Brandon—it took me a while to get to that point but I did get there. And now, after many phone meetings with Jamie, I'm totally comfortable and relaxed talking to Brandon using her as our go-between. I almost feel as if I'm sitting down with Brandon at our kitchen table and talking to him face to face.

But, of course, I'm not talking to him face to face—I can't even hear his voice on the other end of a phone line. Everything he says has to be translated through Jamie, and it's not a perfect process. How could it be?   Jamie has to interpret Brandon's communication through psychic means, has to hear what he's saying using powers most people don't have and that nobody in this world understands, not even her. She sees images on her psychic screen and receives "spoken" messages, almost like listening to a radio tuned into another frequency. When the radio isn't perfectly tuned in, Brandon's messages to me might waver or get a little bit fuzzy. What he's telling me has to make its way through Jamie's consciousness too. And, as she says, Brandon talks really fast and throws a lot at her all at once. Plus, there are other spirits that come with Brandon who all try to talk over each other. Given all that, it's amazing that Jamie does as well as she does. She is truly gifted.

And even though the communication isn't always perfect— it's not really the same as talking to Brandon, just the two of us sitting at home at the kitchen table—I *know* it's real. I know it because I can feel Brandon's presence, during those meetings with Jamie. I can hear his voice in what Jamie passes on to me, I hear his exact verbiage in the messages she passes on, I recognize him in every gesture and mannerism she says she sees when we meet.

My son Cody says the same thing. He's been meeting with Jamie and Brandon too, four times a year since 2010, because, he says, it makes him feel like Brandon is still here, still with him, and that's more valuable to him than anything. The other day after one of his meetings Cody said that the communication isn't always perfect, and that sometimes he feels like he's hearing Jamie talking instead of Brandon. But then, he told me, "Just about the time I think it's not Brandon, Brandon comes through and says something that only he would say."

For example, one day, when Cody was asking Brandon what he needed to do to make his business take off, Brandon said, through Jamie, "Well, for one thing, you've got to quit moaning so much." Brandon used to tease Cody about his moaning when he was alive, and these days Cody's partner Billy complains about Cody's "moaning" at work when he hasn't had enough sleep. It was as if Brandon was referring to that, and Cody knew it had to be him talking.

Although the communication through Jamie might not be perfect, and we only get to do it four times a year, and we can't see Brandon sitting across from us or hear his voice with our ears, it's still, as he would say, a hell of lot better than nothing. *Nothing* is what we had before I was lucky enough to find

Jamie and what most people have after their loved ones have passed. Not only nothing as in there can be no communication, but nothing as in the person himself is nothing—they don't even exist any more or they've gone to some vague place called heaven that's so far away you could never find it or even truly believe that it exists. I never thought that Brandon was nothing after he died, I always had the sense that he was somewhere, but I had no real hope that I could find him, I wasn't sure if he was still himself, and there was some part of me that wasn't totally, 100 percent, convinced that he still existed at all.

Since I found him in the afterlife with the help of Jamie, all of that has changed for me. Now I *know* he's still alive. I feel him nearby at all times. My view of life and death has changed—I no longer think of death as the end but only as a transition to a new beginning—and although I still miss Brandon, sometimes desperately, I no longer grieve his loss in the same way, because I know he's truly still with us, just in a way I don't and can't completely understand.

Chapter 16

Saying Hello Instead of Goodbye

Once, during a session, Jamie said that Brandon leaned back on the couch and said, referring to the way we were talking, "This is how life should be for every dead and living relationship. What the heck is this ignoring [the idea of the dead person], never saying their name again? We should be able to stay in touch all the time. We should just be in conversation all the time."

And a little later he said, "Mom, you should tell everybody that finding a good medium is like trying to find a good lawyer. Everyone should do it."

I'm a little nervous about suggesting that everybody who's grieving should find a medium. That choice might not be everyone's cup of tea, and there may be other reasons, such as financial ones, why it's not an option for many people. But for me, finding a good medium has been a lifesaver and a Godsend. I keep going back to Brandon's statement that finding a good medium is like finding a good lawyer. We spend lots of money on lawyers, therapists, vacations, and other things, and we would probably never let economy get in the way of connecting with the people we love who are still around us. And in the same way, maybe it is worth investing some money in finding and carrying on an on-going relationship with a loved one who's gone on to the afterlife. I know that for me, finding Brandon, talking to him, feeling like he's still in my life, still part of our family, is worth any amount of money.

If you do decide to look for a good medium, I suggest you take your time instead of rushing into something with the first person you hear about. Ask around. Talk to people you trust, talk to anyone you know who works with a medium or who knows someone else who does. You're looking for a medium with a true gift, someone who has the ability to see, hear, or sense the presence of people who have passed to the other side. Collect evidence through word of mouth that any medium you hear of can be trusted and has a track record of accuracy in the messages they pass on. Do they tell their clients specific things they couldn't have known, rather than just generalities anyone could figure out? Don't be misled by people who prey on other people's tragedies by making claims they can't deliver. It took me a year to find Jamie, and what convinced me to call her was my daughter's friend telling my daughter, and her telling me, that he had been speaking to his deceased parents through Jamie once a month for six years. He said what she passed on from his parents unmistakably came from them, and that Jamie was the real deal.

Once you do find a "good medium," as Brandon said, just remember that this kind of communication is not an exact science. Like I said above, by its very nature the communication isn't perfect. Even Jamie, one of the best there is, occasionally says something that I don't connect with. For example, when my friend Kathy and I met with her in Atlanta in 2009, she told Kathy that a cousin of hers who had died in a car accident was there during the meeting. Kathy said she didn't know who that was because she didn't have a cousin who died that way, the reading continued, and she and I forgot about the whole thing. If I had thought any more about it I might have concluded that Jamie had been mistaken. It was only recently that I realized that *I* had a cousin who had passed in a car accident: my cousin Darrell's son, David, had died in a car crash about nine years before the meeting with Jamie, and that must've been who was there.

During any reading with a medium it's important to be diligent about what you're being told, and sometimes you have to sort through the messages to find the truth. On the other hand, you can't always draw the conclusion that the medium isn't legitimately making contact with your loved ones if they say something you don't connect with. It may be tempting to start questioning the medium's overall ability when that happens, but I suggest holding on a while longer, waiting to see what else you get and knowing that something may come to you later that clears up the confusion. You'll know when the communication is really working because it'll be very concrete and you'll know instinctively that the message is coming straight from your loved one to you. That happens with Brandon when I meet with Jamie more times than not.

Once I asked Brandon what advice he had for people who were grieving.

"Well, Mom, it's like this," he said. "People need to learn how to say hello, not how to say goodbye [when somebody dies]. They didn't lose a son or a daughter or a parent. I'm not lost. I'll tell you that again and again and again. I'm not lost, nobody lost me, and I definitely didn't lose myself. So when you talk to people you shouldn't say, 'When I lost my son I...' because that will be inaccurate. You should say, 'When my son passed away.' The word 'lost' no longer belongs in the definition of grief."

But it's not that easy to make the transition from saying goodbye to saying hello, to thinking that there's still someone there to say hello to. We're programmed in our culture and told over and over in every possible way that when someone dies they're lost, they're gone, they don't exist any more. We're even told we need to let go and say goodbye.

But now I know it's not about saying goodbye. I was already fairly open to saying hello instead of goodbye compared to many people, but even I had to set aside my cultural programming in order to let, as Brandon said, "the reality of [him] come in." And now I'm totally sure that when someone dies we haven't lost them.

"What makes it possible for consciousness to survive death?" I asked Brandon. "There has to be a way that it survives without the brain. Correct?"

"Absolutely," Brandon said. "Your consciousness is your soul. Consciousness is not generated by the brain, the organ, but by the soul. If we're looking to boil it down," he said, "the soul has more elasticity than our physical body does. But the soul is trapped inside our body, connected to our body, and when the physical body is functioning, [the soul] can't stretch into other dimensions. It just doesn't have what it takes. When the body is broken and the soul is untethered from those particles, untethered from inside, its elasticity is very, very great. So the soul immediately has possibilities of going into other dimensions."

I found all this very interesting. At first it was hard for me to connect with the word "soul." Soul is such an abstract word— it can mean so many things, and a lot of times when we use it we don't really think about what it means. Then I remembered that Brandon had said our soul is our consciousness—it's who we are.

"[Dying] is almost like setting a dove free from a cage," Brandon said. "It can fly within the cage, but when the cage door is open we have all these other places to go to. But the dove is still the dove. It still remembers being trapped in the cage and what it ate and what it did and who it saw there. It still remembers who it loved and it still loves them. But now it has the ability to go elsewhere. It's the natural state of being for that soul."

"I still think the vastness of all this is so hard for us humans to understand," I commented. Shortly after that it was time for that particular phone date with Jamie to end. "He says he loves you so much...blowing kisses," Jamie said.

I hung up and sat there at my kitchen counter, thinking about how lucky I was to have found Jamie and therefore to have found Brandon. I thought about how different I would have been feeling right now if I hadn't gained all this knowledge and awareness that helped me climb up out of the dark hole of suffering and grief. And I thought about what Brandon had said, that dying is like being a dove set free from its cage though it still remembers its life in the cage. Even though I miss him and can't help being sorry he isn't here any more, in his cage, another part of me has found peace in the thought that he's been set free.

EPILOGUE

THE POEM

I was dozing one morning in early January 2015. Often, right before I'm totally awake, I feel as if someone is speaking to me. I'm not having a dream; I just kind of hear words someone puts in my head.

This is what came to me early in the morning when I was lying in bed on January 12, 2015. I tried hard to go back to sleep but something told me to get up and write down these words so they wouldn't escape me. I got up unwillingly and put pen to paper.

The words that were in my head started with something about a precious gift and how we receive this gift and how some of us are asked to return this gift. My thoughts immediately went to Brandon. I also thought about something I'd heard many times during mass: Words about how God sacrificed his only son, and how that is the ultimate sacrifice anyone could give. At times after Brandon died the thought of that Bible verse made me want to get up and shout, *What about me?* I gave my son! I couldn't understand why I was chosen to sacrifice my son.

I had a feeling of urgency as I wrote down the words that came to me early on that January morning. I knew I couldn't lose them because they were a message from the spirit world and that there was a good chance they came from my son.

I worked all morning putting the words together into a poem. I started the poem at about six-thirty in the morning and finally finished it at twelve-thirty. Here it is:

THE GIFT

There is a gift some are asked to give
It comes from a place far beyond where we live
And oh what a beautiful gift it is,
Entrusted to us for only a while
That gift we received with that beautiful smile
Engraved in our hearts that cannot be erased
The vision of that beautiful face.
Some will never understand the sacrifice we gave
Only our creator had suffered the same.
He called them home, for they are his
And oh what a beautiful gift it is.

After I wrote out the poem I had a feeling of coming full circle on my journey of finding my son. When my husband came home for lunch I asked him to read it to see if it made sense. As he read the poem tears welled up in his eyes. When he finished he said, "It's beautiful. It made me cry."

APPENDIX

Here's a record of some Brandon-sent dimes people have found since he passed away. Brandon always seems to leave the dimes for people who touch our lives, especially those who are having difficulties or who need a bit of convincing that he's still around.

January 14, 2008: My husband's sister Cheryl finds the first dime when we were on our way to the funeral home for the visitation. It was lying on the snow and ice-covered sidewalk.

June 16, 2008: My mom finds a dime in her suitcase when she opened it to pack to come to our house. The suitcase had been empty three days ago after she unpacked it on arriving at my sister's house.   I like to think the dime was Brandon's way of thanking her for traveling from Arizona to Iowa to be there for me as I grieved.

February 12, 2009: My long-time friend Donna receives a dime in a startling way. Her husband Gary had passed away suddenly from a stroke at the age of fifty-eight. She and I listened to her friend Keith do a practice read-through of the eulogy for Gary in her living room; when Keith stood up a dime hit the wood floor.

October 30, 2009: Cody's girlfriend Britni finds dimes all over the place—in her billfold, on her bedroom floor, outside her house on the sidewalk—when Cody's planning to propose at the end of the week. Looking back, Britni said she felt as if dimes were dropping out of the sky, as if Brandon was trying to tell on Cody.

October 31, 2009: Kenny, Brandon's dad, finds a dime on the middle of his closet floor. Sometimes you just know why they are placed there. It was opening day of pheasant hunting season, which is always a hard time for Kenny since he and Brandon loved to hunt with the dogs on Grandpa Smith's farm. With that dime it was if Brandon was saying, "Hi Dad, I'm okay. So please don't be sad."

December 8, 2009: My sister Anna finds a shiny dime beside her pick-up truck when she's leaving to take an important test in nursing school, the night after a snowstorm. There were no footprints in the freshly fallen snow. She called me immediately on her cell phone and I told her that was Brandon telling her she'd pass her test. Of course she passed.

January 17, 2010: I spot two dimes lying in an airplane aisle about a leg's length away as Britni, her sister Lindsay, and I travel to St. Thomas to check out wedding venues for Britni and Cody. I wasn't supposed to be sitting in that seat; a nice gentleman had given me his seat so I could sit with the girls. I saw the dimes as we were about to land, on a very short runway, and I thought, How am I going to reach them with my seatbelt on? The girls were laughing at me trying to dive after those dimes in the aisle while we were landing, even as they were freaking out about the short runway. I finally unbuckled my seatbelt (way against the rules), stuck my leg out as far as I could, and dragged the dimes to me with my foot. When we were disembarking a stranger turned around and said, "Gee, I hope you find some more money for your vacation." The girls and I laughed our heads off. Sometimes I have to risk looking like a crazy woman as I show up for communicating with Brandon.

June 10, 2010: On Brandon's thirtieth birthday, Jackie, the wife of Brandon's friend Bill, encounters ten dimes as she's putting a load of jeans in the dryer. As she was transferring the jeans from one machine to the other the dimes flew out onto the floor. The pockets of the jeans were empty when she loaded the jeans into the washer. It had been two years and five months since Brandon had passed. I believe Brandon was saying to Bill, who was his age, "Hey man, it's my thirtieth today."

August 18, 2010: My childhood friend Karen finds ten dimes in one day, scattered around her house as she cleans while after her youngest child moved into her own apartment. Later she said it seemed like every time she turned around, in every closet, every drawer, every corner, she found a dime. She was the only person other than Bill's wife Jackie to find ten dimes in one day. She freaked out and said to Brandon, "Alright, that's ten. Now go home to your mother." We still laugh about that. Brandon continues to leave her dimes almost weekly. Once she found one stuck in the rubber seal in her freezer door.

November 19, 2010: My good friend Sherri opens her back door in Iowa and finds a large gray toad sitting on her back porch, on the day Cody is getting married in St. Thomas. She swept the toad gently away with a broom and found a dime sitting on the cement where the toad had been. Sherri walked with me throughout my grief journey, never failing to listen to my stories as I told them over and over trying to find a different ending. She continues to find dimes.

January 15, 2011: Kenny's niece Emily sent her father, Kenny's youngest brother Chris, a text with a picture of a dime she had found on the gym floor underneath the bench her team was using during a basketball tournament in Chicago. Fifteen minutes later Emily's sister Elizabeth came over to Chris at the volleyball tournament she was playing in and he was attending—in Minneapolis—and handed him a dime that she too had found on the gym floor under the bench her team was using. Brandon loved sports and he loved Chris, Emily, and Elizabeth. Later on that summer Chris's son Lucas found a dime on the ground by the passenger side door of his dad's car after a Little League baseball game he played in. He had just made the final strike out in the last inning and his team lost the game. I'm sure Brandon was sending his love and saying, "It's okay buddy."

September 2, 2011: I find a dime in a concrete hole in a parking lot shortly after my fifty-fifth birthday. On my birthday I had said jokingly to Brandon, while I was going somewhere in my car, "You know I just turned fifty-five, that is kind of important, don't you think? Please just acknowledge your mother's progress by giving me a dime." I spotted the dime two days later as I was walking to my car after work; by then I had forgotten what I had said to Brandon on my birthday. The dime caught my attention; it was as if it was shining in my eyes. I bent down and picked it up. The date on it was

1980, the year of Brandon's birth. It was as if Brandon was making a joke about his birthday being important too. I put the dime in my pocket, smiled, and said to him, "You got me."

September 10, 2014: My younger brother John finds a series of dimes in the house he bought and started renovating in Newton, forty-five miles away from us. One day I asked him if he had been finding any dimes as he was remodeling and he said no. I asked Brandon to give him some dimes for encouragement— John was working full-time during the day and remodeling the house at night and it was going slowly. About a week after my request John started finding dimes—one in the driveway, one in the hosta plants, three or four inside the house.

January 4, 2014: My mother gets out of the car and sees a shiny dime in the snow between her feet, after getting a clean bill of health following a series of health crises that should have resulted in surgery at best. When her physician learned that the health problem had corrected itself on its own, he said he had never seen that happen before.

August 15, 2014: Kenny's father pries up a wooden threshold in his house and finds a dime underneath. He had crafted the threshold a month earlier and nailed it to the floor but wasn't happy with it. He insisted that when he nailed down the first threshold there wasn't a dime under there. When I talked to Brandon through Jamie the next time after that, Brandon said, "I nailed it," when Grandpa Smith's name was mentioned.

ACKNOWLEDGMENTS

I would like to thank my husband Kenny for his undying love, support and encouragement, and my daughter Jessica and son Cody, for being patient with me in my brokenness as we suffered through the loss of Brandon. I'd also like to thank my daughter in-law Britni, who stood beside me every step of the way, gave me love and support, and brought the two most beautiful rays of sunshine into this world, McKinli and Calvin.

My thanks also go to our extended family for surrounding us with the support and protection we needed. They are the definition of family: a circle of strength and love.

I'd also like to express my profound gratitude to all of my truehearted friends who came to my rescue, picked up the pieces of my shattered world, and walked with me throughout.

Thanks also to Father Nick and Steve Witt who were instrumental in guiding us back to the light of God's love. Our family will be forever grateful for their guidance.

It has been my privilege to work with Mary Allen, my writing coach, editor, and friend. I could have searched the world over and never found someone who was such a perfect fit for my book. In her nonintrusive way she gave me the confidence to dig deep in myself, and my memories, allowing me to put my heart and soul on the pages. She helped me capture Brandon's spirit on the page, showing the wonderful, fun-loving, truehearted person he is. For that gift alone I will be forever thankful. As we worked together we continually felt Brandon's energy and presence, contributing to the book in his own way.

Thanks also go to my therapist Jessie, who helped me believe in myself and become stronger than I had ever imagined I could be. She genuinely trusted in me and gave me guidance to find the tools I needed to love myself and honor my son's life.

I'd also like to acknowledge graphic designer, Todd Bakir Wali, who designed the logo on the book for publishing, my web page and business cards. His constant attention to my needs will not be forgotten. I'd also like to thank his sweetheart Monica who is always and forever an angel. Their abilities and acts of kindness, freely bestowed on our family, will never be forgotten.

To Charles Eicher, design services, for formatting the book and cover design with his special talents and attention to detail. I will be forever grateful for your help and assistance.

My heartfelt appreciation goes to Jamie Butler, the wonderful clairvoyant who helped me find my son in the afterlife. Her gifts are remarkable, especially because they are used to show kindness and compassion to others.

Last but certainly not least, my thanks go to my beautiful gift, my son Brandon. The life lessons he has taught me have taken my journey to a whole new level. Brandon, I know you will be proud of the words on these pages. I will never stop loving you, my Beautiful Gift.

ABOUT THE AUTHOR

Lesa Smith is a registered nurse in a small town in south central Iowa. She is accomplished in many areas of the nursing profession, including internal medicine, oncology infusion, and college nursing. She feels very blessed to be the mother of a daughter and two sons, Jessica, Brandon, and Cody. She and her husband of forty years, Kenny Smith, live on Lake Ponderosa in Montezuma, Iowa.

She felt a passionate desire to pass on the true story of the tragic loss of her middle son, Brandon, in 2008, in the hopes of helping other parents who have suffered the same.

CREDITS

The text of this book is set in Adobe Caslon Pro with Minion Pro ornaments. Graphic design by Charles Eicher and Todd Bakir Wali. Cover photo by Britni Diane Smith. Author photo by Jo Jones. Printed and bound by Sutherland Printing in Montezuma, Iowa.